MW00929006

Agency Success Roadmap
Your Personal GPS to Agency Success

Copyright © 2018 by Lee Goff

All rights reserved. No part of this book may be reproduced or transmitted in any form or by any means without written permission from the author.

Printed in the USA

Agency Success Roadmap

Your Personal GPS to Agency Success

TABLE OF CONTENTS

Agency Success Roadmap
Your Personal GPS to Agency Success

Preface

Why did I write Agency Success Roadmap? I wrote this book to provide a real-world roadmap that empowers both existing and future agency owners with a proven system that allows them to scale and grow rapidly. All of this is intended to help them achieve their version of the American Dream, so they can spend more time with family and friends.

This book is intended to act as a "Stratagem" or "Roadmap" to construct the agency of you always dreamed of.

A stratagem is a plan or scheme, especially one used to outwit an opponent or achieve an end. I am in business for one reason: to serve agency owners just like you, to give you a plan, a blueprint, a roadmap that is why this book is a proven roadmap to financial success.

This book came about after building my own multi-million-dollar agency, the stress from accomplishing that goal literally almost killed me.

Everything I learned while building that agency, has been tested by myself and my team and distilled down into a step by step process or in other words a stratagem for you to build your very own agency.

Now, using the information within these pages, in 365 days (or much less) you can change your business from lacking the focus to a laser targeted profit pulling machine.

You're about to learn about the most useful strategies to grow, scale and finally ENJOY your digital marketing agency.

It's going to be your secret weapon to stand out from the competition. Along the road to completing this book you will find Helpful Hints and Map Markers for insights to give you the extra inspiration to finish this road trip to success.

In my world, it's all about RESULTS.

That is why myself and my team focused on one single question throughout the completion of our courses, tools, books, webinars, blogs and everything we produce: *Will this get fast results and make the lives of agency owners easier?*

This book answers that question in the affirmative.

I truly hope you can use every morsel of knowledge in this book to achieve success in your digital marketing agency because I want you to have all of the information, tools, and systems that are required to build a successful agency without spending 15 years and millions of dollars learning it the hard way, as I did.

"Before hiring Lee, I was a taskmaster, now I own my marketing agency, and I am a true marketer! Life transformation!"

~Laura Kamrath
Pres. Zebra Marketing Solutions

"Before hiring Lee I had done 174k in business over 3 years, after hiring Lee I closed 500k in residual contracts in less than 60 days."

~Brennen Bliss
CEO Pixel Cut Labs

About the Author

Hello, I'm Lee Goff. And I'm in business to do ONE thing: *Make Agency Owners Lives Easier!*

While building my agency, I would have given almost anything for a book like this one.

A roadmap that could provide the exact path & steps I needed to grow my agency faster, with more efficiency and less stress. Plus be able to run it in a way that did not require everything to be tethered to the agency owner; like it was in the first years of my agency.

After spending 13 years founding, building, scaling, retiring from and then successfully exiting my digital agency... I took a year and along with two full-time employees did vast amounts of research and testing on exactly what tools, templates and system delivered results for all agencies. From there we stressed tested all programs with real-world agencies across the world, fine-tuned it, and....

I really want to hit home how important what you will be getting with this book, so I want to tell you my "WHY" ...This gets personal.

After suffering a severe heart attack in June of 2016, I took some time off to recover and spend time with my daughter.

I very soon got back on the saddle and began creating the world's best resource for other marketing agency owners.

That was accomplished by spending an entire year locked up in my offices with two full-time employees researching, writing, creating tools (over 75 of them) and formalizing proven systems (the roadmap) that can be easily transferable to other agencies throughout the world.

I mean... I know what worked for me at my agency, but I wanted to know for certain if that knowledge transferred seamlessly and would it be the best for other agencies to follow, also.

After my research and testing it with my employees, I then launched the program, and real-world stress tested the roadmap with my one-on-one coaching students for over a year.

What you are reading in this book is the latest and greatest roadmap that we developed after 13 years of ownership, 1 year of research/program/roadmap creation and 1 year of extensively stress testing everything in real-world scenarios.

You see, the stress that I endured while growing my agency had a direct impact on why I had a heart attack.

At the age of 43, that and the small business diet (whatever you can find and eat FAST) almost cost me my life — almost taking away God's precious gift of raising my beautiful daughter, being with family and simply enjoying life.
I am on a mission to help as many agency owners as I possibly can, I do not want one single agency owner to experience what my family and I experienced.

The primary reason I was so stressed is that I was flying blind. Meaning, I did not have a roadmap to follow. It was a daunting challenge to figure out what tools and systems I needed and when I needed them.

This book is the aggregation of me setting off on that higher purpose at the beginning of 2017 and continuing until every single aspiring agency owner, or experienced veteran agency owner has their shot at living the American Dream. If you follow this roadmap, you can achieve the personal satisfaction of starting, scaling and eventually selling your agency if you so desire.

I hope you enjoy it, and most importantly I hope it gives you a few items you can implement today that will improve the quality of your health and/or life!

Nothing but the best,

Lee Goff

P.S. Thanks for reading. Now that you know all about me... you get to reap the rewards of our blood sweat and tears!

So, regardless of what types of services you offer or niche you serve, if you follow the steps in this book, your agency will run substantially smoother, it will generate higher profits, and it will allow you to delegate *with confidence while spending time with friends or family. And please feel free to call at any time – we love to help our Agencies!!*

844-409-0994

Lee's Agency Experience (2003 - 2016) Biography:

Since founding GetUWired in 2003 in Lee's upstairs bedroom, GetUWired has helped thousands of business owners around the world break through the glass ceiling and live the lives they deserve — making more money with less work and having more time for all the things they love. Lee is living proof that his formula works.

In 2013, using Jim Collins and the Infusionsoft's leadership team as his inspiration, he began handing off leadership responsibilities, eventually leading to his retirement from that company in May 2015.

In May 2016 he sold out his remaining shares to his longtime partners to pursue his lifelong passion of mentoring small businesses. His motto is *"Success using vision, leadership and shared knowledge."* He shares everything he learned while building GetUWired. His new venture is marketingagencycoach.com and is in business to help small businesses grow faster and more profitable than they could have ever imagined.

A few of Lee's Accomplishments (While Running GetUWired):

- Founded GetUWired – Digital Marketing Agency – Infusionsoft's #1 App Sales, Revenue Producing and Done For You Implementation Services Worldwide. Built this company into a multi-million-dollar organization that he eventually retired from and sold to his longtime partners.

- One of the lead consultants to the country of Fiji's tourism industry, Lee was instrumental to the team that increased the entire countries GDP by over 5% in 12 – 18 months.

- Lee has personally consulted two ICON Ultimate Marketers of the Year finalist, with one of those clients winning (It is like winning the Oscar in the Infusionsoft ecosystem).

- Entrepreneur Magazines Small Enterprise Top Company Culture in the US, one of 25 companies to receive this prestigious award.

- 2015 Elite Business of the Year Finalist – Infusionsoft (Infusionsoft has over 120k clients worldwide)

- Guerrilla Marketing Master Trainer

- Infusionsoft Certified Partner

- CEO - Founder - MarketingAgencyCoach.com

"Lee built the first scalable and "real" agency in the Infusionsoft ecosystem. "

Clate Mask, CEO & Co-Founder Infusionsoft

Introduction

This book is an agency roadmap that helps you travel down the road to success. You can use the express lane and finish as quickly as you can. However, I recommend you stop at each attraction during the ride, so you can master each skill before tackling the next. This book is designed so that with a month of action taking and implementation you can master each chapter. You will learn a lot by just reading this book through, but if you have the discipline to get the 12 systems, processes and tools I mention in this roadmap implemented, you will become a Successful Agency Business Owner with enough profit to pursue all of your life dreams.

The principles and strategies written in this book are timeless and not limited to a specific agency model. These tactics are proven and have worked for startups and medium-sized agencies. It's worked for all types of agencies as well: Creative, Advertising, Development, Social Media and Media Buying agencies.

I've laid this book out so that you can work on each chapter at your own pace. **For the purposes of this book, we recommend a month for each chapter**. If you are a startup with a ton of time on your hands, you can get it done a lot faster. If you are a medium sized agency with employees, a month or even longer may be required. Rest assured that If you follow the roadmap, you can expect to accomplish the following items for your agency...

- **Niche your agency into a target audience** that can afford your services and you enjoy working with.

- **Get Productized.** Have a fine-tuned product line of services that allow you to charge value-based prices while continuing to offer custom solutions to your clients.

- Create an overwhelming competitive advantage over your competitors. **Learn about your leads**. Know exactly where, when and how to always get more leads/clients.

- **Become a thought leader** in your specific niche, allowing you to charge much higher prices, speak from the stage and drive higher quality leads into your agency.

- **Learn to delegate and make the right type of service framework** - Have all project management processes completely standardized. Begin with the end in mind, if a product is sold your service department should be empowered with an entire framework that walks them step by step through the deliverable process.

In other words, become the best and ONLY choice for your target audience.

So, from picking who you will target to getting the targets to see you as their only real option, we've got it covered in our month-to-month roadmap to becoming a highly profitable agency!

Learning is improved by changing tasks each hour, spreading the work over time, and dipping into it more frequently.

A Harvard Study found that many people can read for about twenty minutes without losing concentration. Because of this information, this book and it's *corresponding courses/programs are sectioned into easily digestible pieces that will help you learn what you need without taxing your ability to absorb the material OR hinder your time.

*Anytime you see an asterisk beside a resource, you will be able to find more information on that topic at the end of this book under the RESOURCES section.

So, to get the most from this book…

Plan your actions

Begin with the End in Mind **+** Have a **plan.**

Think things through.

Do one thing in the right order before you need to do the next thing **in order** to get where you want to go.

Always **work on items that will free your time** up going forward. I call these *infrastructure items*; these items are setup one time and then they run on their own.

At first it is as simple as automating your follow up, then you create a product that can be sold thousands of times and it continues from there.

If you begin with the end in mind, plan your actions, take small steps consistently towards your goals you can and will achieve your version of the American Dream.

MONTH ONE

During this month's "travel" you will focus on "how to" tap into the best niche for your agency. You will receive simple and practical information to assist new and existing digital marketing agencies to choose the right niche for growing your agency both strategically and exponentially.

Chapter 1

Your 10 Step Niche Process

In this chapter, you will learn about the benefits of picking a niche for your agency and how to vet and select the right niche so that your agency can experience incredible, predictable, and reliable growth.

It seems like all of the sudden we're seeing information about niches everywhere.

It's all "Find a niche." and "Niche Down!"

Have you ever thought to yourself...?

"Should your agency be full service or niche?"
"Will picking a niche really change anything?"
"How do I handle my existing clients?"
"Do I REALLY need to niche out?"

If you haven't yet asked yourself these questions, **then you should** be.

Why are niches such a big thing all of the sudden? Ever hear the phrase "history always repeats itself"? Well, it is true.

As we've seen throughout history, when an industry is created for the very first time, it takes time to figure things out and perfect them, but once that industry has it figured out - everyone hops on board and makes it more and more precise to solve specific pain points in specific industries and to solve specific pain points.

Let's look back in time to just before the industrial revolution.

Henry Ford famously said in the early days of the Model T, "*You can have any color Model T you want, as long as its black*."

Flashback to when they dreamed up assembly lines, and for first time began to produce hundreds of cars a day. Then, your options were limited because he was literally figuring everything out for the first time. Today, and you can have any car in any color you want, with custom interiors, custom dashboards, custom everything. You're no longer limited to a black Model T because he developed the core systems, processes and tools required to mass produce a car for the middle class. Once he did, he and his competitors could optimize the assembly line to deliver more and more focused products that can now literally satisfy any buyers personal requirements.

Let's look at another example, in the early 80s there was no such thing as digital marketing. Then the digital revolution happened, and web marketing was born, that's right it was called web marketing for years, then it was internet marketing and now it has finally settled on digital marketing.

At first AOL was the big dog search engine, then Internet Explorer and of course now Google dominates that space. For the first 10-15 years of the internet, digital marketing was still in its infancy, so your options were limited. Fast forward to today, your possibilities are endless because people have started to crack the code. I refer to this as "the dust is settling" phase of our industry. As the dust settles and we are given the foundation to deliver better and better services, it will become more and more critical to niche down to remain competitive.

So that is a little of the history as to why you are hearing more and more about finding a Niche. When you settle on a niche; it will accelerate your growth, improve your quality of work, make your prices more competitive, increase your profits and deliver substantially more value to all of your clients.

By finding a niche, you can create a digital marketing strategy and products that are 100% customized to your client's individual pain points. No longer is either party limited to a black Model T.

"FINDING A NICHE ACCELERATES YOUR GROWTH, IMPROVES YOUR QUALITY OF WORK AND MAKES YOUR PRICES MORE COMPETITIVE."

Well, you start by picking the right niche for your agency. This decision determines your trajectory and where you land so it essential to choose the right one.

That is why I wrote this chapter because you need a system designed specifically for agency owners like yourself.

This chapter will guide you through the critical decision-making process, help you define your niche, get you in front of your niche, and start you down the path of creating your products.

Whether you've been in business for six weeks or six years you should know exactly what your target audience looks like. Your audience should be who you like working with, who your best clients are, and who you want to work with in the future; <u>not</u> the next person that will give you money.

There might be a couple of different industries, sizes, and types but you should have a general idea of what you're working with and after you decide on your niche, that task becomes ten times easier.

Ok, let's get started down the road of niching your agency. In the next few pages we will go over the 10 Step System

1. DIGITAL FRIENDLY
2. COMPETITIVE ANALYSIS
3. TARGET AUDIENCE DEFINITION
4. TARGET AUDIENCE FINANCIAL ANALYSIS
5. NICHE OPPORTUNITY SCOPE
6. LONG-TERM GROWTH POTENTIAL
7. GENUINE CARE
8. GETTING IN FRONT OF PROSPECTS
9. UNDERSTANDING THEIR PAIN POINTS
10. HIRE A COACH

that maps out picking the perfect niche for your agency/lifestyle.

Write what you already know down; *this is your starting point.* Either use a notebook, excel sheet or some other app to get this accomplished.

Once you know which niches and audiences you currently work with or you'd like to work with, it's time to determine if they're a good fit.

Step 1:
Get Digitally Friendly

Is the industry niche you are choosing digitally friendly?
A lot of industries have done as little as possible to embrace
the digital world - believe it or not they still exist!

Make sure the industry you're going to target doesn't
intentionally run from digital marketing services. If you pick
an industry that avoids digital marketing, then every day will
be an uphill battle (*and it doesn't have to be!*).

Are they *digitally adverse*; meaning does the industry have a
tendency to like or dislike the digital world? or are they
digitally inclined; meaning that they are ready to embrace the
digital products you're providing?

Step 2:
Competitive Analysis

Who else is doing it? You're probably not the first person to
consider this niche so you need to find out what you're up
against. And think, if no one else is in this niche, why?

Research the **top 3 competitors** and compare what they're
offering to what your agency is capable of offering.

Now if you do not currently have all of the capabilities of your biggest competitor, do not let that discourage you.

Everyone starts somewhere and with the white label service providers on the market currently, anything is possible.

See where their strengths and weaknesses lie and make sure your agency can stack up to the competition or can find the resources required to compete.

Remember, NEVER let your competition dictate how or what you do.

You're here to be unique and it's ok to blaze a new trail and change an industry, just make sure the industry is ready for it.

- Harvest the top 4 competitors for review
- **List out their product lines**, list them in order of popularity (*Do the best you can*).
- Research their most popular products
- Think "do they have products or do custom services?"
- Figure out **how long** they been in business.
- Discover how long have they been serving that niche?
- And do they serve **more than one** niche?

Stop to take a moment to think about what makes you unique and put it down in a list
BEFORE
you research the top 3 competitors and compare what they're offering to what your agency is capable of offering.

AND REMEMBER
NEVER let your competition dictate how or what you do.

STOP
TO THINK

RESOURCES

Check out the Resources area for how to download the **Agency Niche System – Data Harvesting Spread Sheet**.

Step 3:
Target Audience Definition

The first step to making a HUGE impact on your niche is to provide customers with personalized messaging to let them know what you're offering to them and how it solves specific pain points they are currently experiencing. However, you can't refine your messaging if you don't know who you're speaking to. Start by defining your Ideal Customer Avatar.

- Who is your perfect client?
- What do they look like?
- Where do they look for answers or ask for help?
- What keeps them up at night?
- Can they afford your services?
- What conferences or continuing education sources do they attend?

Give your Customer Avatar a name, a story, and a personality. The better understanding you have of who they are, the easier it will be to reach them and connect with them.

There are hundreds of target audience worksheets on the internet, some are good, and some are bad. We have a very detailed version in our coaching programs, but regardless of how you organize your thoughts, find a way to document and organize your thoughts around your target audience.

Step 4:
Target Audience Financial Analysis

A need and desire for your services aren't enough... unless you plan on working for free. You need to make sure your target audience has enough money to pay for premium marketing services.

Some industries are booming, but their profit margins are so small that they don't have the budget to spend 10-12% on marketing initiatives. Unless you're okay with slim margins too, think very hard before entering into this type of niche!

Everyone debates, and it is different for different industries, but healthy marketing budgets normally hoover around 10%.

If any of the industries you are hoping to target cannot afford or will not spend in the range of 10% on their marketing efforts annually, it is typically a safe bet to go in a different direction.

Find an industry that on average spend around 10% on their marketing budgets annually.

THINK: Do they make enough money to pay for high-end digital marketing products? If not, are you willing to make small profit margins? (*This will inhibit your growth tremendously.*)

Step 5:
Niche Opportunity Scope

Is the niche so new that no one knows it exists?

Is it so popular that it would cost a fortune to break through?

There might be a lot of opportunities but if you're up against large established agencies you might never stand a chance.

Alternatively, you might pick such an obscure and narrow niche that people just don't need your services that much.

Make sure there are **viable** opportunities right now.

Here are the top things to consider:

- What is the current opportunity?
- Have the competitors been growing?
- Are there new competitors?
- What are the competitors charging for their services?
- Are the annual conferences averaging at least 500 people?
- How many publications are serving your possible niche/industry?
- Is the industry new or has it been established for a long time?
- What are the industry projections for growth over the next 1, 3, 5 and 10 years? (If available)
- Monitor social media trending, is it growing or declining?

Step 6:
Long-Term Growth Potential

You need businesses now but you're also going to need it in 6 months and in 6 years. Do your research and make sure your niche will provide a healthy flow of opportunities long-term. Ideally, there will be more opportunity long term because the niche is trending and growing. If you want to grow and scale your agency, the industry needs to be growing too.

Step 7: Genuine Care

No research for this one, just some soul-searching. **Do you genuinely care about the industry, products, people, etc.?** Of course, this is not an absolute or hard-core requirement, but it definitely makes life easier. You won't always be motivated to work so hard but if you genuinely care about the industry and enjoy the work you're doing it will be easier to push through the tough times.

Step 8: Relationship Building

How do you get in front of your prospects...? One of the benefits with focusing on a niche is the fact you can build a reputation in a specific industry. Building a reputation allows you to build long term relationships that lead to speaking opportunities, guest posts, podcast, backlinks and more. In chapter 6 I go over traffic generation ideas, with a specific niched out target audience, it becomes easy to get in front of your ideal prospects.

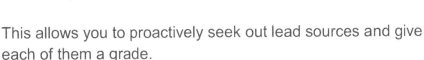

This allows you to proactively seek out lead sources and give each of them a grade.

I personally go to at least 3 or 4 new events each year in an attempt to see what is out there and form new relationships.

Below there are a few things you can do to get that process started.

In this step, you should have a spreadsheet with at least:

- 4+ events you can attend each year for lead harvesting

- 3+ possible referral partners (businesses who are paying to acquire your target audience but with very little to no competitive overlap)

- 6+ directories, associations and of course paid media channels like Facebook/Google

- Industry specific publications with monthly newsletters, mailing list, etc.

- Sponsorships Opportunities

Step 9:
Understand Their Pain Points

Can you really relate to the pain points of the niche?
Yes, understanding your niche's customers' pain points is key to making your agency stand out.

You think of it in this way and you will start to see… 90% of all digital marketing services are identical across industries. Videos are videos, blogs are blogs, ads are ads.

It's the remaining 10% that makes agencies and industries so vastly different. This 10% stems from understanding your target audiences pain points and seeking out solutions that provide relief or open up new opportunities.

Does their pain come from not having enough time?
Then create products/services that make their lives easier and get results.

Does their pain come from another agency's screwing them over? Then they're looking for someone to get the job done right but understand you will have to earn their trust first.

Does their pain come from not knowing Adwords? Then give them a Google Adwords product list, make it EASY for them to spend their hard-earned money with you. .

If you truly understand your target audiences' pain points and you create products that solve those pain points, the selling process becomes more of an order taking process.

When you can fine tune your product offerings over time, you eventually end up with a product that delivers overwhelming value/results and takes your agency very little time to implement.

Let me give you quick example:

Let's say you provide digital marketing services to *underwater basket weavers* in California.

One of your clients said they wanted to test out Google Adwords. Once you take the time to research the keywords, negative keywords, extensions, write the ads and design the retargeting ads then you have a proven foundation.

You take that foundation and test it for months, fine tuning those keywords, adding negative keywords, sculpting the ad copy to convert and over time you have a converting machine.

Now that you have perfected the process, bundle it up and sell it to other underwater basket weavers in different parts of the state or in other states.

It would take you a few hours to roll the entire campaign out, you can charge premium fees and your clients will love you because you are dropping leads into their systems.

That is a win-win-win for everyone, and **this win-win-win for everyone** would have never happened if you never focused on a specific niche, understood their pain points and sought out solutions (your products) that easily solved those pain points.

Taking the time to intimately understand your target audiences pain points will pay off huge dividends in the long run. It shows you genuinely care, and you genuinely can relate to how they feel.

In today's world of fake feelings, when you are speaking from a place of genuine care, people can tell, and they will naturally gravitate towards your message.

 Find their pain, understand it and you'll find success.

Step 10:
Hire a Coach

At the end of the day, there is no substitute for having someone **who has actually built a successful agency** in your corner.

I've seen the good and bad side of picking niches. I've experienced all the highs and all the lows. Owning and running an agency is one of the loneliest places I have ever been, get an experience sounding board and stop living on that island yourself!

As much as your significant other, employees or friends attempt to relate, until they have walked a mile in your shoes, it is just not possible to understand the pressures of running a digital marketing agency.

It's astonishing the difference it will make in both your professional and personal quality of life.

There is no substitute for experience...

10 Step Niche Process Wrap Up

Now, just follow this 10 Step Niche Process, you will find your niche and your audience.

Once you have your niche in place, you will be ready for the next step in creating a profitable agency.

Next Up, How to Create Your Products......

MONTH TWO

In the following chapter, you will learn to create a product out of any skill, knowledge and/or prototype service using Productization.

Chapter 2

It's All About Productization

Having a niche audience willing to spend money is not worth anything if you don't have something to sell. Get ready to use your skills and knowledge to create your products using my "blocks" Productization pricing model

WHAT IS PRODUCTIZATION?

So, WHAT IS Productization exactly? AND *why should you care about it?* WHAT IS PRODUCTIZATION?

So, **WHAT IS Productization exactly?** AND *why should you care about it?*

Ok, let's start by getting the right definition. According to Investopedia and from my research the best definition is this one...

"Productize" refers to the process of developing or altering a process, idea, skill or service to make it marketable for sale to the public.

When something has been productized it means that it has

been taken from a raw or minimally developed idea and has been turned into a standard, fully tested, packaged, supported and marketed product.

For example, a person can productize their expertise by creating a product or service based on that knowledge. To productize is not the same thing as the production of a good or service.

Productization does not involve a tangible, physical good. Rather it is an idea, a process, a prototype, an area of expertise, or skill that has been developed (or productized) into a marketable and salable product.

Services may be productized, packaged and sold just like physical products.

For example, a marketer can write a "how-to" book for new entrepreneurs that would teach them how to market their business, web designer can create a DVD series on how to design websites or savvy agency owners can sell predefined products (Google Adwords, Lead Magnet Templates, Websites, etc..) that provide overwhelming value and take considerably less time to implement.

Productization is a key strategy in creating and running a service-based business.

We will cover the systems you have to have in place to successfully build or transition into a truly productized agency business, BUT THIS IS NOT A DEEP DIVE INTO EACH SYSTEM, that takes time and is unique to every agency.

One of the many amazing things about this model is that you determine exactly what you want your products to look like based upon your desired lifestyle choices.

So, if you want to keep it simple, develop 2 or 3 products and rock them out, now if you want to go bigger and more complex, then so be it. **Provide products for every possible pain point in your specific niche, <u>own it</u>!!**

The 6 SystemsTo Productize Your Agency

All of the information you are about to learn has been in the works for 15 years, I have been personally testing this productization model with dozens of my one on one coaching students to get this implemented for them.

The results are ABSOLUTELY AMAZING, REALLY LIFE CHANGING, and REALLY ABOUT TO CHANGE THE GAME FOR THE DIGITAL AGENCY INDUSTRY!!!

It increases profit by at least 15-25%. When you Streamline the deliverable process by up to 30-50%, it is easy to see how your profits can double in some cases.

You can now have a technical task list

Every time you deliver one of your products you can double check the quality against the checklist and if anything does not come back to your expectation levels, you modify the technical task list to adapt for that quality assurance issue and **BOOM, it is fixed forever!**

Now, imagine once you get it perfectly dialed in, now you can tarball it and deploy it thousands of times going forward. You literally just cut the workload by half (if not more) on that project this time and every time going forward.

Now apply that to Adwords, Facebook Ads, Marketing Automation Campaigns......**the applications are limitless.**

That is how you get higher profits out of Productization. You raise your prices via a value-based pricing model and cut deliverable cost by at least 30-50%,

Ok, so now that we know what Productization is and why it is important, what are the exact 6 systems required to get your agency productized and streamlined for sustainable growth?

Rope

Rope (tow rope) stands for having a common thread - When you have something on a rope, you begin with the end in mind. This applies to Productization for an agency, here is a simplified example of how this should look after it is in place.

First, you hook them up and get them into your systems.

This is commonly done with lead magnets, call to actions and so on... You are likely to be familiar with this process, however, if you are not you can find more information in our courses as well as in the chapters Month Five and Month Six - *Next, comes the proposal.*

Everything in the lead magnet will set the first impression and expectation levels around what you say in the proposal and all documents that come after.

After you make the sale, the scope document should be in perfect alignment with the lead magnets, proposals and all service documents that come during the project and are required to effectively deliver on what you promised.

In today's "Shiny Object" society people are more and more sensitive to anything that does not feel right to them. A lot of times they might not know why it does not feel right, but they just know it is not in alignment with what they are searching for and therefore will not return your calls, emails, etc.

If you can get your entire product line in alignment with all of your messaging, meaning everything is on a rope, then your close percentages will sky rocket and so will your profit margins.

If everything aligns and the client receives overwhelming value. Just like if you tow a car... If it is aligned, you get where you are going.

If you are aligned, then you just created a raving fan that consistently delivers new clients into your lead funnel and at that point, the entire process starts over.

It is predictable, reliable and requires substantially less time from you to deliver overwhelming value every single time you sell one of your products than it does to deliver overwhelming value for custom work.

Blocks

When I was young I played with a really cool set of toys. These toys allowed me to build shapes with different colored blocks that can be easily snapped together. You know the type that kids leave all over the floor, the colorful interlocking plastic bricks - they come in different brands...

Now, for legal reasons I won't mention the brand I had as a kid, so for the purposes of this book we are going to refer to them as "Blocks". **Now, it is important to remember that**

these are very special blocks, for example these blocks can:

- Be Different Colors

- Be Used To **Build Anything** You Can Dream Up

- Allows Your Prospects And Clients To "**Build Their Own** Perfect Hybrid Super Car"

- Can Be Different Sizes

- Can Bolt Onto Each Other

- Can Be Used Individually Or As A Combo

And for example, purposes these super special blocks will represent individual products. The blocks or products range from a discovery phase to a website, ChatBot, organic SEO, design products and any range of services *so* blocks, and products are the same things, they represent the building blocks for all services your agency provides.

And when you build your products in an object-oriented fashion, each object can stand on its own two feet or be combined with any other objects and sold as a combo product, therefore empowering your agency to build out custom solutions for prospects and standardize the entire service framework that delivers reliable and predictable results every time.

 Ok, so blocks are *not impressive by themselves* unless you step on one in the middle of the night!!! Then you literally end up crying on the floor like a baby.

Ok, that is an exaggeration, but I am sure we would all agree that <u>one</u> block is NOT impressive.

However, if you take your blocks and put them together, they can build some pretty amazing things. Give 25 identical blocks to 20 different kids and you will get 20 different results. The 20 kids all used identical blocks, but each built something completely different and each of their unique creations are special in their eyes because they personally invested in the building process.

Simple but effective, and unique to each person, one can use blocks to build whatever they dream up.

Similarly, **it's like helping a client buy their very first custom-built new car**, when they go into the dealership they start with the base model. Then they go through the process of customizing their new car and when they walk out, in their mind, it's unlike anyone else's car in the whole world. They feel pride in it, they tell stories about it, they will have a picture of it to show their friends and even complete strangers walking down the street.

Now the reality is that there are probably thousands of cars like yours out there, but when you play a part in the building process of the blocks, it is unique and special to you, and that is all that counts!

That is how the client feels about your solutions for their business when they can pick from core blocks (products) and can then customize them with add on blocks (products).

Your blocks should be based upon specific pain points your niche's target audience experience on a regular basis.

Create blocks for your prospects to play with, let them dream, let them build their own *digital marketing supercar with **your blocks***.

Your prospects will thank you as they drive around in there new high-performance marketing supercar.

Your clients, employees, bank account and family will thank you as well!

Service Framework

You must have a standardized system that delivers predictable and reliable results **every single time** you sell one of your products. An important aspect of the Productization pricing model is this:

Once you get the individual blocks set up in a truly object-oriented fashion, at that point you can then create combo packages from your individual blocks.

Just about EVERYONE makes the mistake of going with larger packages as your products, this is wrong and will not fix anything, all this does is keep you in the same custom work cycle that everyone else is stuck in.

When your products are broken down into individual objects that your service department can proactively plan to deliver, you are now empowered to build any combo package you want (as long as you stick to your blocks) and your service department will simply know it as multiple blocks and know exactly how to get it implemented with almost no help from you.

This requires *Scope documents, technical task list, swipe copy, templates, change order docs, legal agreements,* basically everything your agency needs to deliver your products and services without you being personally involved in the process.

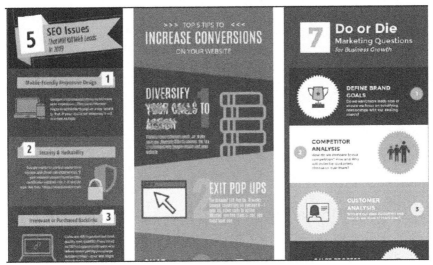

It all starts with **the lead magnets**, now I just said service framework, so why am I talking about lead magnets??

BUT BUT…They have nothing to do with service!!

Yes, yes, they do! The lead magnets should be setting the tone for everything else.

They set the tone for Proposals

Proposals set the tone for the Project Scope Documents

After the scope document is presented and signed off on, the team gets started with their *standardized task list*; now this is in excel, why would I say to have a master technical task list in excel?

Why not just build them in your PM task tool or board?

It is critical that leadership has a version that remains the master task list. When QA issues pop up, test them out in the PM task tool or board before changing the master task list.

This document is intended to maintain the leadership control and integrity of the process.

Remember, once you create a process in the Project scope document, the team will become comfortable doing it that way.

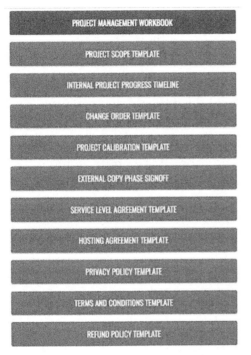

Once the master task list is fine-tuned and you are confident in it to deliver predictable and reliable results, you should treat any changes to the master task list as amendments to a constitution (big deal).

You will need time to prepare materials, notify team members and so on before things just disappear and appear on their task list.

Ok, scope template, change order, project calibration template, phase sign off documents, legal agreements and so on.

It sounds like a lot of work, and it can be if you do not have the templates, agreements, blocks, etc. So, make sure to check out www.marketingagencycoach.com for templates, tools, online courses and the Agency Success Roadmap Group Coaching Program.

But, once you get the first product done, the rest of them go by very fast.

Next thing you know, you have some happy customers playing with their blocks and you are cashing checks!

And after you are done with a block/product, you create a folder with all of the documents on a rope for each product.

As soon as you sell a block/product or a combo product, you submit the order to the project manager; they open up the product folder and begin the predictable and reliable process of over-delivering value-based products to all of your happy clients.

Visualize something like this...

That is such a glorious feeling when you finally achieve the point that when you sell it, you do not have to worry about it again.

Glorious feeling for sure!

Value Based Pricing

Value-based pricing is an instrumental part of productizing your agency. By default, you will establish a value-based pricing model with your products when setting up your blocks.

When you **develop your products in the 'blocks' pricing model** format it allows you to build it once and sell it thousands of times.

Every time you sell a block and your team delivers it, you can fine tune the process to deliver that block/product. So not only are you delivering overwhelming value to your clients, you are also providing them a custom solution that fits their exact requirements and it takes you substantially less time to deliver.

You see in the blocks format you not only make more profit on the sell price; the real profit is in you optimizing your delivery processes of which we will cover later in this book.

This will impact the custom work as well, but in a way that will have a *very positive* impact on your pricing.

You see when you have products, and everything is clearly defined, you have no problem putting your prices on your website.

You want to put the prices on there because it sets the tone for everything your agency does. If someone wants custom work, and they have already seen the product prices, it is perfectly logical to assume that custom work will cost a lot more than a product price.

Simply by rolling out your blocks you will increase your billable rate for custom work as well.

Bespoke Equals Broke

This is one of the fun sayings we say in our coaching calls. I would like to get T-Shirts done and send them to my students, give them away at events and so on!

I am not a fan of custom work every time you get a client, The point of productization is NOT to 100% eliminate custom work, but the point is to mitigate it as much as possible.

If you are doing custom work, you are leaving a ton of money on the table.

Productization delivers more value, for less effort and a cheaper price, it is a NO BRAINER for your agency and your prospects.

NOTE: If your purpose is to work one-on-one with clients and get heavily involved in the creative process, then productization is not for you. You should then **focus more on your brand positioning** elements than productization, this will allow you to raise your billable hour to a profitable level.

Existing Clients

Typically, you will do a slow bleed out to your existing clients. Meaning you will introduce the new products to them as they inquire about them.

Now, this does <u>not</u> mean you do not attempt to drive interest, include it in your newsletter, etc.

When transitioning former clients there are creative ways to introduce the new product line to your existing client base, again this is not being forced on them.

They have the option to continue on the same plan they are on or move over to one of the new products. You will find that most of them will be very receptive and see the value in the new product line.

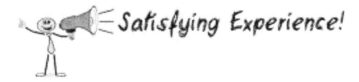 Satisfying Experience!

A few creative ways are "Free Giveaways", that gives them one of your new products for free. Let them test drive it, they will become receptive to the new product line and you are solidifying that client relationship going forward.
Or you can invite them for a customer appreciation dinner and have a small presentation for them, again the ideas are limitless, at the end of the day. It is not as big of a deal as

you might think if you have a plan in place and handle it properly. Creating a satisfying experience helps them to remember you and your agency.

As you go through this process you will find that you will lose a few old clients, this is perfectly fine because you will be making more money per product sold as a result of the switch.

Productization Wrap Up

Now, just follow this 10 Step Niche Process, you will find your niche and your audience.

Once you have your niche in place, you will be ready for the next step in creating a profitable agency.

This chapter has taught you how to turn whatever you're good at into something scalable, now that month two is over you should have a product in mind ready to be packaged up and presented to your specific niche.

Ok, again the point is not to eliminate custom work.
The point is to limit it to less than 25% of the work done by your agency.

Look, you know, and I know that if you are doing custom work for every single project, you are ultimately swapping time for money.

Even if you are billing $150 - $200 an hour, you are still swapping time for money and your profit is fixed, your ability to scale is extremely limited.

Productized agencies will dominate their niches within the next 3 – 5 years, if not a lot sooner. You better get ahead of this industry trend, or it will get ahead of you.

MONTH THREE

In the month ahead, you will learn the powerful outlines for mapping out proposals, so people can really see what your agency can do for them.

Chapter 3

Proposal Delivery System

Having a productized agency and having niche who needs you is a great MAP for a successful agency. However, people need to know how wonderful a DRIVE you've mapped out before they will be willing to invest themselves in your agency.

The PROPOSAL

We all know that not every proposal is created equally. Some prospects want a simple brochure-type website, some prospects have no idea what they want, and others have an advanced RFP (Request for Proposal) document created.

I have a proven way to land big projects and eliminate 90% of your competition. It's so simple and effective you will kick yourself for not knowing it sooner.

I landed tons of 20k+ deals with less than an hour of proposal creation time in my first agency using this proposal outline. And now I am sharing that outline with you. **Check in the resources area for a link to where you can get a *writeable proposal template.**

An outline for your proposal should include:

Guiding Philosophy - Branding/brand penetration, why do you do what you do?

Definitions - Explain marketing terms.

Define target audience - Research on who the client is trying to reach and what their needs are.

Outline existing assets and processes - BRING THE PAIN. Remind them that what they're currently doing isn't working, this builds a case for why they need you.

Strategic recommendations overview - Big picture overview about why you're recommending what you're recommending.

Project Timeline – Outline the specific phases of the project.

ROI projection - Associate this to real world increases in traffic/leads/revenue/profit. Current versus projected.

If you're dealing with an **Advanced** Prospect, here's your proposal outline

Digital Marketing Proposal

(This proposal template is for a comprehensive digital assets management project – A prospect looking for a digital agency to take over all aspects of their digital footprint)

Always have a formal footer at the bottom of every page. Never make them look for contact info; additionally, brand penetrate every chance you get.

Programming – (EXAMPLE COPY) (WordPress, CMS, Custom Apps, etc.) – We pride ourselves in writing nothing but the cleanest and highest performing code. Not only is our code some of the cleanest in the world, but we also write it in a way that makes it user-friendly for both your prospects and your staff to use. We know how critical it is to have internal staff maintain the majority of your digital systems, with our agency, you can rest assured that the training, day to day management and long-term maintenance will be planned out from the beginning and executed to your exact specifications. Upfront Capital Investment and ongoing retainer/residual investment – Outline how much this is going to cost.

Frequently Asked Questions - Settle their hesitancies before they have them.

How To Move Forward With The Project - Some agencies prefer to have all of the legal jargon in the actual proposal where they can sign and engage on the spot. I prefer to reference the legal jargon on your website to keep the barrier to entry as low as possible. (yourwebsite.com/legal, yourwebsite.com/sla, etc.)

Executive Summary - This is where you wrap everything up with a pretty little bow and tell them how stupid they are if they don't move forward.

Personalize – Do NOT simply mail this to your prospects, you must personally present the proposal to the prospect and only after you have presented it and framed the entire proposal, you can send them the proposal and always make sure you get a next action date. If you can use an online proposal management system, do it!

Close The Loop Management Systems - (EXAMPLE COPY) At its core, a closed loop management system means that all data from point of contact, sales process and order taking are all tracked in great detail and each order processed can be traced back to the exact point of initial contact.

This is generally done in one CRM system, but it can be accomplished via multiple systems.

Even though it can be done in multiple splintered systems, it is best to have one centralized cloud-based CRM platform that allocates for lead nurturing, sales pipeline tracking and order processing.

This allows for real-time KPI dashboards that empower your organization to react to opportunities in real time.

Brand Penetration – (EXAMPLE COPY) The name of the game is to get your brand identity in front of your prospects in a high value manner as often as possible.

The reason Fortune 500 companies spend billions of dollars a year on advertising is to penetrate their target audience's subconscious with their brand in a high value or emotional manner.

There is a simple formula my marketing mentor taught me: If your prospect has been touched by your marketing efforts on average 7-9 times, their opinion of your agency is a positive one, and most importantly, your brand has now been transitioned from short-term memory to their more trusted long-term memory.

This way, when they are in the market for your services, they will recall your agency's brand, pick up the phone, and reach out to you.

Definitions

(Most organizations don't use marketing terms on a daily basis; give them a quick reminder of the terms used in the proposal)

Digital Assets - Digital Assets represent the goods sold by an organization or they are in themselves among the goods being sold, their value usually increases according to their usage. Digital assets can be reused as is or with minor modifications over time. A few examples of Digital Assets are as follows: domain names, images, multimedia, email lists, target audience data, digital documents (PDFs), Digital Marketing Collateral (Postcards, Re-Printable Materials), Online Training Portals, Websites, Landing Pages, Advertising Copy, etc.

Mind Map – A visual representation of complex processes. Mind maps outline the flow of processes or marketing campaigns in a simple to understand visual format. All processes/marketing campaigns should be mind mapped prior to engaging any paid resources (copywriters, programmers, designers, etc.)

Lead Magnet/CTA – Call To Action – Any item that asks your prospects or clients to take action. The most common are "Call Now" or "Click Here". These Calls to Action are critical to any success formula and special attention must be given to all CTAs. Successful business owners understand the value of testing CTAs constantly.

Best Management Practices (BMPs) – Methods or techniques found to be the most effective and practical means of achieving an objective while making optimum use of the firm's resources.

Key Performance Indicators (KPIs) – KPIs evaluate the success of an organization or of a particular activity in which it engages (marketing campaigns, sales rep performance, lead sources ROI, etc.)

Level of Effort (LOE) – All time, money and resources it takes to accomplish a specific task, goal, milestone or project. LOEs are normally more successful if the business owners understand that there is at least a 10% variance and the value of quick decision-making in all LOEs.

Customer Acquisition Cost (CAC) – Refers to the resources that a business must allocate (financial or otherwise) in order to acquire an additional customer.

Content Management System – (CMS) – The platform a company uses to implement, optimize and syndicate content to the Internet.

Target Audience

(These are generic examples of how to define your prospect's target audience. Use the most relative items that your prospect identifies with as their ideal client)

HELPFUL HINTS: Insert a brief write up about their target audience behavior at the bottom of this page.

Create an Avatar if you have time, give it a name and let the prospect know that we are targeting (Insert Avatar Name). Everything you do will be to get more (Avatar Name)'s in the door.

AGE – INSERT BASIC AGE RANGE

NAME – INSERT BASIC OVERVIEW OF AN IDEAL CLIENT, SOMETIMES USING AN AVATAR IS A GOOD IDEA, JUST MAKE SURE YOUR PROSPECT KNOWS WHAT AN AVATAR IS FIRST.

GENDER – INSERT BASIC OVERVIEW

HOBBIES – INSERT BASIC OVERVIEW

INCOME – INSERT BASIC OVERVIEW

GEOGRAPHICAL LOCATIONS – WHERE ARE THEIR IDEAL CLIENTS ARE LOCATED

NUMBER OF EMPLOYEES – IF YOUR PROSPECT IS B2B, INSERT THE AVERAGE NUMBER OF EMPLOYEES THEIR IDEAL CLIENT NORMALLY HAS.

NET INCOME PER HOUSEHOLD – IF YOUR PROSPECT'S IDEAL CLIENT IS B2C, INSERT THE AVERAGE MEDIAN HOUSEHOLD INCOME.

Outline of Existing Sales and Marketing Digital Systems

(This is when you bring in the pain. Explain to them how their existing systems are underperforming, and dramatically hurting the marketing department's performance/conversions.

The example below was custom for a specific prospect. You should make this generic and comprehensive at first, then you can simply delete the sections that do not apply to a specific prospect's needs.)

HELPFUL HINTS: I would pay close attention to the first few minutes of the introduction call. They normally will mention two or three things that they want to fix. These are their primary hot buttons.
The copy below should cater to those hot buttons.

If you get access to their Google Analytics or can install Usability software (HotJar, CrazyEgg, etc.) you should take some high pain point screenshots (like 404 errors, web forms that are not working, etc.) and insert them into your proposal for larger projects.

WEBSITE OVERVIEW:

Currently (INSERT PROSPECT'S NAME) is using an HTML based content management system and the time it takes to manage this system (third party vendors) and the functionality it provides is outdated and needs to be updated. Websites need to be a truly responsive, dynamic and able to be managed in house without having a programmer to implement the most basic items such as a call to action, blog post, social media shares and split testing efforts.

BRAND IDENTITY OVERVIEW:

Currently (INSERT PROSPECT'S NAME) brand does not represent the future of the company. Although this brand has served the company well as it established credibility in XXXXXX industry, leadership recognizes the value in updating all branding assets with a more modern image that represents what (INSERT PROSPECT'S NAME) evolved into and where it envisions itself in the foreseeable future.

Strategic Recommendations

(When you read below, you will notice the content below is very high level and does not get into great detail. Focus on the big picture in this section; lay out the vision for the next 12-18 months. You do this to see and prepare the client for a long-term commitment with your agency.)

During the investigation phase, the obvious issue is the outdated CMS, lack of conversion tactics, lack of follow-up procedures and lack of paid media. Understanding that the goal is to eventually close the loop between marketing and sales, doing this with the existing infrastructure is going to be very difficult, if not impossible. I recommend implementing the following digital infrastructure items in two phases.

Design new brand identity. This will include the website, landing pages, ads, email templates, etc.

Implement Rebranded Website into a user-friendly Content Management System (CMS).

Research Customer Relationship Management (CRM) Platforms.

Implement CRM (Infusionsoft/HubSpot, etc.) for centralized data management and automated follow-up capabilities. Design and Implement target audience specific landing pages.

Design and Implement target audience specific automated follow-up campaigns.

Design and Implement an automated sales pipeline management system.

Establish key performance indicators (KPIs) to track the success or failure of specific media buying campaigns, etc. Research and launch media buying (Google Adwords, Facebook, Instagram, etc.) Establish media buying and landing page split testing procedures. Test calls to action, taglines, etc.

PHASE 1 – Primary rebranding, infrastructure build out and customer relationship roll out. In this phase, we will rebrand all aspects of (INSERT PROSPECT'S NAME) digital assets to convey a professional and strong brand identity across all platforms.

PHASE 2 – Design, setup, and roll out media buying (advertising) channels, establish precise KPIs for leadership to monitor performance, setup optimization (split testing) procedures, and maintain digital infrastructure.

Project Timeline

(This is a big picture overview of expected timelines. Consider it a general guideline of how the project should flow from a strategic level. Make sure to give time buffers on all phases of at least 20-25%. It is okay to deliver early, but never okay to deliver late.)

PROJECT PLANNING PHASE   1 – 2 Weeks

Finalize project scope document, mind maps, set up project management portal, train all parties on the process, harvest critical login credentials (domain name, Google, etc.).

CONTENT WRITING PHASE   3 – 4 Weeks

All content must be completed and approved by the client prior to any design working be done.

DESIGN PHASE   2 – 3 Weeks

Create a concept for all pages involved in the project for client feedback and approval

PROGRAMMING PHASE   5 – 6 Weeks

Engineering all aspects of the project, coding custom features for content management system, landing pages, lead source tracking, split testing, etc.

FUNCTIONALITY TESTING, CROSS BROWSER, AND FINAL EDITS PHASE   1 – 2 Weeks

Present the working concept to your client for final edits and functionality testing. At this point, the project should be 99% completed and the client should have minor tweaks.

WARNING: this is when scope creep usually happens, be prepared to handle this with change orders.

GO LIVE AND TRAINING PHASE   1 Week

This is when you have final sign off by the client and are ready to push all aspects of this project live and hand off responsibility to the client.

MEDIA BUYING AND OPTIMIZATION PHASE
Ongoing

We write ad copy, produce creative assets for Google, Facebook, Instagram, etc. We begin running paid traffic to all digital assets and monitor conversion rates on a weekly basis.

Return on Investment Projections

(This section does not always apply. If you are building a website, this section will most likely not apply. If you are driving traffic and can get current media buying, conversion percentages and customer lifecycle value this section does apply and can separate you from your competitors.)

HELPFUL HINT: This section does take a little extra work up front, but if you are working with a large client that can potentially be large monthly residual paying client; it is definitely worth the additional effort.

Based upon our research of your existing media buying platforms (Google Adwords, Facebook, etc.) we project an increase of XX% over your current traffic levels.

Currently, you are driving XX leads a month with your existing media buying efforts. Our projections show that we can increase this by XX% and potentially lower your monthly media-buying budget by XX%.

Existing Lead Flow and Revenue

Existing Lead Volume	Existing Sales Close Percentage	Total Sales per Month	Customer LifeCycle Value	Total Monthly Revenue
100 Leads a Month	30%	30	$10,000	$300,000

Projected Lead Flow and Revenue

Existing Lead Volume	Existing Sales Close Percentage	Total Sales per Month	Customer LifeCycle Value	Total Monthly Revenue
125 Leads a Month	30%	38	$10,000	$375,000

Existing Gross Revenue
$3,000,000

Projected Annual Revenue Increase with our Program
$900,000

Project Gross Revenue with our Program
$3,900,000.00

With your existing sales closing percentage being XX%, we project the following increase in revenue over the next XX-XX days.

Based upon our projects, of which are based upon the lead flow, sales close percentages and customer lifecycle value provided by INSERT PROSPECT NAME. We estimate an increase of XX% within XX months of implementing our media-buying program.

Capital/Ongoing Investment

(I found that if you position the upfront build out phase as a capital investment instead of a marketing budget line item it helps to close the deal and can open additional funds for the project.)

PHASE 1 – CAPITAL INVESTMENT $32,000.00

Design Website Concepts – Up to 30 Pages
Design Landing Pages – Up to 5 Landing Pages
Write Website Copy
Setup Staging Server
Install CMS
Implement custom website concepts – custom HTML, CSS, Java, etc.
Setup Google Tracking – Analytics, etc.
Setup Usability Tracking – HotJar, CrazyEgg, etc.
Setup Split Testing Tracking Platform
Activate Infusionsoft/HubSpot CRM
Implement automated follow-up sequences
Implement automated sales pipeline management system
Setup Google Adwords Campaign
Setup Facebook Ad Campaign

PHASE 2 – MONTHLY/ONGOING INVESTMENT $2500.00

Set Up KPI Dashboards
Monitor Google Adwords
Optimize Adwords based on KPI Data
Monitor Facebook Ads
Optimize Facebook Ads based on KPI Data
10 hours of digital infrastructure modifications and maintenance
Monthly performance reporting on media buying channels

Frequently Asked Questions

(These are examples. Think about the top 5-7 questions you get asked after delivering a proposal and place those in this section of your proposal. This shows you're on top of it and it also provides clarity to your prospects. This can also cover you legally in certain situations.)

CAN WE DO ANY OF THIS OURSELVES?

Of course, you can, but in our experience that has a tendency to slow things down and increase the budget. We have developed a streamlined process that keeps things moving. Our copywriters work closely with our designers to ensure everything fits perfectly. When someone with no experience writes copy, it normally slows down the entire process, therefore slowing down our ability to produce higher quality leads for your organization.

CAN WE HOST THE SITE OURSELVES?

We strongly recommend you do NOT. Hosting is a very complex process and if your website goes down in the middle of a large media buying campaign the minimal cost saved is dwarfed by the revenue lost in lead generation. Also, most companies are not equipped to manage a dedicated server, security patches and firewalls required to maintain a stable and secure website hosting platform.

WHAT ARE THE 4 PILLARS OF BRANDING?

The four pillars of branding is a common technique used to identify the framework for a successful rebranding project. Some agencies use different definitions for the four pillars, but we use these four. Differentiation, Relevance, Esteem, and Knowledge. Once we determine what these four pillars mean to your organization we can effectively begin to design a world-class brand identity.

HOW LONG BEFORE WE SEE MORE LEADS?

It depends on the details of the Infrastructure Build Out, but on average it takes 90 days. If that is the case, we will have new traffic coming to your site within 2 weeks of the "Go

Live" date and leads will begin to increase at that point and continue to increase until you tell us you have too many leads. ;-)

HOW DO WE GET STARTED?

To move forward with this project, please do the following items:

Sign the bottom of this proposal and get it back to us. (If you use an online proposal system, ask them to click the execute the proposal via that proposal system.)
We require an XX% retainer fee to be paid prior to any work beginning.
If you are ready to move forward, but have a couple of changes to scope, schedule a meeting with your sales representative. Please note that any substantial changes to the project could increase the cost of the project.

When we receive the signed proposal and the XX% retainer fee, we will schedule a project discovery and transition meeting. In this meeting we will introduce you to your team, train you on critical systems, review your proposal and begin the process of developing a detailed project scope document for us both to work from.

We pride ourselves on over delivering. With this in mind, you will have a dedicated project manager you meet with regularly to discuss wireframes, color pallets, design concepts, working prototypes and anything relating to the project as it is outlined in your proposal and scope document. We also provide a cloud-based project management portal that all files, login credentials, and communications will reside.

We do all of this to make your experience as positive as possible.

If for any reason you feel your project manager is not being responsive enough or not delivering what you're expecting, we also provide the ability to escalate this project to his or her boss and we guarantee that these meetings will be 100% confidential and handled with discretion.

This hardly ever happens, but it is nice to know that you can go straight to the top in case something does happen.

Legal Stuff - Get Started

(Some agencies like to put all of the legal copy in the proposal; I have found that to be a substantial barrier to entry. I prefer to reference the legal copy we have posted on our website and provide links for them to review.)

DISCLAIMER: Obviously I am not an attorney, so consult with your attorney if you have any questions about how to best handle the legal aspect for your agency. The cold, hard truth is that if the client has an issue with your services, it will cost you more to fight it than it will to settle it, not to mention the bad public relations/reviews you could potentially get.

If you decide to place the legal copy in the proposal, make sure you cover all possible services you are offering for this project.

This should be standardized, and in language that is easy for them to understand. Please understand that you can have fancy legal copy that is prepared by the best lawyer in the world, but if the prospect/client "feels" like they are not receiving value or have been done wrong, there is nothing to stop them from filing a lawsuit against you, leaving negative reviews about your agency, or talking negatively about your agency in your niche/community.

At all costs, you should mitigate all negative client experiences and do everything you can to ensure they leave happy at best, or at worst, satisfied with a mutually beneficial settlement agreement.

The Most Common Services Agencies Provide:

HTML/CSS CODING – Define what this means to your agency and make sure they understand what it means.

CUSTOM PROGRAMMING – PHP, ASP.net, Java, etc. - Define what this means to your agency and make sure they understand what it means.

DESIGN – Define how many edits they get before being charged additional fees.

PLATFORM PLUGINS – WordPress, CRM, API Coding, etc.

Automation Campaign Setup

PHOTOGRAPHY – Client is responsible for providing royalty free photos or will pay for you to purchase photos.

COPYWRITING – If it is not mentioned in this proposal, it is not included in the price.

TECHNICAL SUPPORT – Make sure you define what is included in your proposal. For example, we fix any bugs for 10 days after go live, etc.

TRAINING – We provide X hours of training on the CMS/CRM/Custom applications, etc. Any training required after the X number of hours will be billed separately, etc.

GO LIVE – During the go live process, we will make sure your emails are working, cross browser, etc.

CROSS BROWSER – We do not cross browser for anything earlier than Microsoft Explorer 7, etc.

There are tons of example contracts if you Google search: "*Digital Marketing Project Contract.*"

Here are some of the more comprehensive ones.

https://www.jonathanlea.net/2013/free-digital-marketing-agency-terms-and-conditions/
https://stuffandnonsense.co.uk/projects/contract-killer/

Again, there are hundreds of templates out there. Get one and customize it to your agency's specific service offerings if you cannot afford an attorney.

Now, if you can afford an attorney, do the same thing and then get your attorney to review it before posting it on your website or in your proposals.

Whether you decide to put the legal terms in your proposal or not, you should always define the payment terms in your proposal.

Payment Terms

(Below are my suggested Payment Terms – of course if your payment terms are different, please be sure to change these.)

50% Retainer
30% Upon Beta Delivery

20% Upon Go Live

Monthly retainer fees begin upon the Go Live phase.
[INSERT ORDER FORM LINK]

HELPFUL HINT: I like to insert an online order form for them to process the 50% retainer fee. Always think about how you can remove barriers to entry without opening your agency up to liabilities. You can always refund the retainer fee if they come back with any scope changes before they sign the proposal.

SIGNATURE AND DATE

SIGNED FOR [INSERT PROSPECT NAME]
SIGNED FOR [INSERT AGENCY NAME]

DATE

__Time is important__ in business and if you want to save time, look in the resources area to find out how to get an editable __Proposal Template__.

Executive Summary

A few things to consider for this section:
This is your last chance to WOW your prospect with your philosophy, awards (insert awards in footer area if you have them), social proof and social trust items, etc.

This section should wrap the entire project up into a simple to understand recap. When writing this section, try to think as if the person reading this proposal has never talked with you and is hearing about this project for the first time.

It should outline your dedication to their success and their ability to always contact leadership with any questions or concerns.

It should remind them of *why* they contacted you for a proposal (their Pain Points) and it should clearly outline the solution you have proposed.

Make sure to paint a clear and compelling picture of what their business will look like after you go live with their website, automated campaigns, media buying campaigns, etc.

If you have ROI projections, you should include them in this section again, and it should remind them of how much money they have lost (or would lose) if they choose to not implement your suggested recommendations.

It should explain that someone in the leadership position has reviewed this proposal and approved everything. This only applies if you have more than one person in your sales department.

It should thank them for the opportunity to earn their long-term business and you look forward to partnering with them to grow their business.

Have a personal signature: Write something that they personally mentioned during the negotiation phase.

We wish you and (HUSBAND, WIFE, PARTNER, etc.) well,

Your Signature

* To help you grow your agency check the resources area to get more information on where to get the tools and services to get you through this process quicker.

Proposal Delivery System Wrap Up

 You've had a month now to practice crafting the perfect way to propose your agency to the perfect client.

You are (Or should be) ready to provide a stellar pitch to the niche you own. You have become the king of your niche in the eyes of your prospects.

Now go out there and close some big deals!

MONTH FOUR

Now is the time to delve into the 'highway' of your sale strategies by working on your elevator pitch, sales deck & proposal deliver system. These are important building 'blocks' and the basic tools you will need to engage prospects.

Chapter 4

Prospect Engagement

This chapter will explain how to create the basic tools to engage prospects, determine interest level, vet on pricing and establish a rapport.

Obviously, you will need lead sources, I cover that more in Chapter 5, in this chapter I am going to give an example of what should happen when you first engage with a prospect. Whether it be on the phone, at an event or via a video conference this simple prospect engagement process.

3 Primary Steps To Engagement

1. Elevator Pitch
2. Sales Deck
3. Proposal Deliver System

As you know Step #3 is so important, I dedicated an entire chapter to that topic alone, (see above). In this chapter we are going to cover the elements you need to understand to create an effective elevator pitch and sales deck for your agency.

Both of these tools are considered "Basic Requirements" for an evolved sales team.

They are part of an overall system that can predictably generate leads and reliably produce profit for your agency. The more you can standardize and streamline the new client engagement process the value of your agency goes up. Take these tools, use them and fine tune them for your agency over time.

Before we dive into the specific pieces of the elevator pitch and sales deck, I would like to give a quick example of how they work together.

When you are meeting a prospect for the first time, we all have certain questions we want answered before we can make an informed decision on our interest levels.

The elevator pitch is intended to break the ice, give very basic information about you, your company and your solutions. **It should take 30 seconds or less.** Once you determine they do have an interest, it is time to determine the level of interest and isolate their specific pain points. That is when you introduce the sales deck.

You have a physical copy and of course a digital copy, you can pull it out at events or present it via screen share.

The presentation is intended to explain more about you, your company, products, experience, etc. It is typically 12 - 20 PPT slides and should not last any longer than 5 - 10 minutes to present.

At the end of the sale deck presentation you ask them if they saw anything they like and if they would like to receive a proposal or more information on specific products/solutions. At this point you schedule a full meeting, typically an hour long to dive into the specifics of their pain points.

At that point you let them know you will generate a proposal and have it ready to present to them within 3 - 5 business days.

Ok, this is a simple example of how this process should flow, now you can use this one or get creative and adapt it to your agencies messaging.

Get these tools in place and practice them on every prospect, every time you deliver it you will fine tune your messaging and increase your sales close percentages. Practice makes perfect, roll up your sleeves and start to practice your prospect engagement process!

In the next few pages, I will breakdown the key pieces to a successful elevator pitch, and then I will breakdown the sales deck puzzle pieces.

Definitions:

Elevator Pitch - A short and persuasive sales pitch intended to be delivered in the time it takes to ride an elevator (30 seconds or less).

Sales Deck - A presentation that provides more information about your products, services, people, experience, and other key sales factors to your prospects/clients.

How to craft an elevator pitch.

Well, at this point there have been thousands of books, videos, white papers, etc... done on how to create the perfect elevator pitch and the impact it has on your bottom line.

No one argues that having a proven elevator pitch can be a game changer for your agency. In this chapter I am going to break down the basic elements you will need in your elevator pitch. As humans we all have very basic needs before we can trust someone enough to give them our time or money. This chapter will provide those basic elements, and as critical as those elements are, they are only half of the fight as it pertains to proving your elevator pitch (prospect pick up line basically) in the real world.

The second half is HOW you deliver it. It is critical that you deliver it with confidence and you gain confidence through practice.

Once you have your elevator pitch written out, practice it in front of a mirror (or while driving), to other prospects, etc.

When you are done, you should be able to recite the elevator pitch in any scenario with overwhelming confidence.

As you deliver it, **pay attention to how your prospect respond to it**, as you test out different words you will notice different responses. When you get a buzz word that gets the reaction you desire, then adapt your elevator pitch and move forward.

It is a constant fine-tuning process, just like split testing a landing pages or ads. The more you do it, the better the results get. Do not be afraid to mix it up a little, throw in some shock value, emotion, etc.

Here are 6 different sections that can be added to your elevator pitch. You should test different variations of your elevator pitch using different pieces, wording, etc...

Sections Of An Elevator Pitch

Who You Are?

Hi, I am Lee Goff, CEO/Founder of MarketingAgencyCoach.com.

What Have You Done?

I founded, retired from and sold my 7 figure agency before the age of 43.

What Do You Do? - Why Are You Important To Them?

We focus exclusively on serving the digital agency community. Our agency specific tools, experience and programs make agency owners lives easier.

Identify Your Ideal Client

Our roadmap was designed to act as a GPS guide for the startup agency to the low seven figure agency.

Industry specific knowledge:

Understanding the difference between billable and non-billable is one of the most important KPI's an agency should track.

Next Steps:

Nice to meet you, if any of this is of interest with you, I would like to schedule a time to discuss your specific situation.

* This meeting is when you present the slide deck. The slide deck will educate them a little further on your company and products. (See how more in resources area at the end of this book)

Here is a complete example of an elevator pitch for my business using different sections

Hi, I am Lee Goff and I am the CEO/Founder of MarketingAgencyCoach.com.

After founding, retiring from and selling my seven-figure digital agency, I dove head first into providing agency specific tools and programs that make your lives easier.

We have programs that work from start up to seven figures, if any of this sounds of interest to you, I would greatly appreciate the chance to schedule a follow up call?

Tips On Delivering Your Elevator Pitch:

- Do not talk to fast

- Be Positive

- Do not ramble

- Have a handout or business card ready

- Do not take too much time - It is called an elevator pitch for a reason, **you have 30 seconds or less**!

Sales Deck

Sales Deck - A presentation that provides more information about your products, services, people, experience, and other key sales factors to your prospects/clients.

Here are 11 critical elements you need to think about when creating your sales deck:

• **Agency Introduction** - Insert your agencies tagline, logo and
any social proof/trust items you have.

• **Your Philosophy** - Prospects prefer to buy from someone serving a higher purpose other than money. Define "Why" you are serving this niche/industry. This is where your agency narrative should build credibility, trust and prove beyond a shadow of a doubt that your "Model" is a superior model for them.

• **The Problem** - Define a few common pain points in your Industry/Niche. Make sure to pick 2 or 3 that the majority of your prospects will relate with.

• **Value Proposition** - Define the value proposition for your agency.

Example: I am in Business to Serve Digital Agency Owners Only…We do this by combining real world experience with real world tools tested continuously in our agency think tank (Active Students)

• **The Competition** - Define what your competition does and why how you do it is better.
Example: My competitors are attempting to serve every small business that will pay them; we put all of our efforts into serving only your specific pain points.

• **The Team** - People like doing business with people they can relate to, show them the owners and possibly a couple of key team members (like Project Managers...) Experience, Skills, Certifications, Degrees, etc.

• **Success Stories** - Give one or two examples that the majority of your prospects can relate to.

Example: After going through my coaching program, Brennen closed over 500k in new business and to create a proposal took less than 3 minutes to complete.

• **Examples of Your Work** - Insert some campaigns, designs or mind maps to visualize the quality of your work and your attention to the details.

• **The Solution (Your Products)** - Your solutions should solve the pain points you mentioned earlier.

• **Wrap Up** - Wrap up the presentation with a 30-45 second recap of the high value (emotion) points about the brand, products, solutions, etc.

• **Next Steps** - Ask your prospect if they can relate to any of the presentation and if so, what parts? Are your services something that they would be interested in learning more about? Once you've completed your sales deck presentation you will **need both a printed and a digital version** of your sales deck.

Prospect Engagement Wrap Up

You have a month to perfect your deck and elevator pitches. Use every minute. It is that important.

Drink plenty of water and get practicing! And you will also need to practice delivering your sales deck like you did the elevator pitch. Good luck.

MONTH FIVE

In this chapter, I am going to show you how to stabilize your lead harvesting efforts. We are going to cover how to diversify your lead magnets, create lead magnets and ensure you always have a steady flow of leads coming in.

Chapter 5

Lead Harvesting

Ok, we have our niche, products, proposals and sales engagement ready to go. Now we need prospects to use all of this stuff. In this chapter we do not discuss "Traffic Generation", we cover that in the next chapter. These two items are confused a lot of the time, the truth is they are two completely different things, and both should have their own individual plan. Both should get scored individually, meaning you score the traffic sources on the quality of people they are sending to your website and you score the lead magnets on how well they convert the traffic once it is to your website.

It never fails: the overwhelming majority of agencies I come across, ask me "how do I get more leads?"

Well first and foremost, you need to – and listen closely here – get out of your own way.

Yes, get out of your own way... Normally, if an agency is not generating enough leads, it's because of the mindset of the agency owner.

As an owner, you have preconceived ideas of how you should get leads and what you should do with them after they get them. This leads to the idea that you'll get leads naturally as a result of your high-quality work.

While this may be true to a certain extent you'll never get enough leads to grow your agency past the 7-figure mark by sitting around with a great product waiting for people to come to you.

Forget about all of the preconceived notions you have about how to get leads and what to do with them.

We'll get into the specifics more as we go through this workbook, but to start you need to learn some of the relevant best management practices.

Step 1:
Getting Out Of Your Own Way

1. BE PROACTIVE

If you're scrambling to get a lead, that's a big problem. You should constantly be harvesting leads from your website, from events, social media, paid media or other offline efforts and be putting them into your marketing database. This way, when you need more leads you can pull from the massive database you proactively invested into building.

2. DIVERSIFY

You must always have at least 4 or 5 proven lead sources that provide a consistent flow of traffic every week and every month. We talk about this in more detail in our Traffic Generation course, so make sure to check it out.

3. NURTURE

Once you have a marketing database with a few hundred or thousand prospects in it, you have to provide high-value content. By providing high-value content over time, you can easily separate your agency from other agencies in your niche or local market.

Never let a lead fall through the cracks, they should be put into an automated campaign and nurtured indefinitely. Check out our Sales and Marketing Automation course for a detailed guide on how to best nurture your prospects at every stop in the sales pipeline.

Although it isn't a "best management practice," the sales pipeline is a visual representation of the traditional paths a prospect takes during the sales process. **This is a critical part of successful lead harvesting.**

Having an established sales pipeline means you, sales reps and management will know how many leads there are, where they are in the sales process, and how much revenue they can expect to generate from them in the next 30-90 days.

(Pipeline chart for reference) opportunity lmvs left voicemail

Step 2: Diversify Your Leads

If you make it your mission to get diversified lead sources in place your agency will explode. Then, you can focus on closing more of those leads by increasing your brand positioning and following a strict sales pipeline process.

Once these items are in place, you'll have so many interested clients that you'll be able to raise your prices, be selective on whom you work with, and still have a waitlist. It is a wonderful feeling to know that you have so much business coming in that the only hurdle to your growth is your ability to scale your service bandwidth.

It all starts with you, the agency owner, making the mindset shift to focus your efforts, resources, and time into establishing proven, diversified, and converting lead sources.

Why is Lead Harvesting Important?

Years ago, I had the honor of being mentored by the father of Guerrilla Marketing, Jay Conrad Levinson.

Jay Conrad Levinson personally taught Steve Jobs, Bill Gates and Michael Dell in some of his classes at Berkeley. Needless to say, this was a life altering opportunity. Not only does he get some credit for laying the foundation for those amazing companies, he also helped to create household name brands such as Starfish Tuna, Morris the Cat, Jolly Green Giant, Marlboro Man, Playboy Bunny and countless others.

At his private events, I would learn so many amazing strategies and tactics -- it was mind blowing, but the best nuggets I got out of those events would be over dinner and drinks after the event was completed.

We would sit on his back porch overlooking the St. Johns River and Lake Monroe discussing marketing strategy and how it applied in the digital marketing industry.

One evening he told me a story about the activity of your typical target audience behaviors; it stuck with me and still holds true to this day.

It's a simple formula that all agency owners should learn and live by.

At any given time, only 4% of your target audience will be ready to open up a dialogue and kick off a project in the next 30-45 days.

These are hot leads in the buy phase, and if you get one, be sure to give them special attention.

Then, there's a second 4% of your target audience that's just started to look around and will be ready to open up a dialogue in the next 45-90 days.

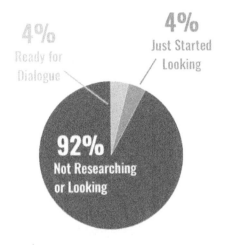

These leads are in the research phase.

Then there is the remaining 92% of your target audience that's not researching or actively looking for services.

That really helps put things in perspective, but it's still not the most interesting part.

The thing is, most agency owners hyper focus on the 4% in the buy phase because those are the ones that are going drive revenue in the next 30-45 days. **But successful agency owners focus on the 4% in the research phase** and the remaining 92%.

Fortunately, this is 96% of your audience.

There's a limited amount of people in your target audience.

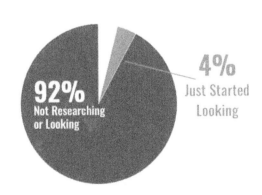

The sooner you can get in front of them, harvest their contact information, and begin the education and trust building phase of marketing, the more successful you'll be long-term.

If you have leads from your target audience in your marketing database and you're constantly adding value and nurturing them, when they're eventually ready to talk, you'll be the first agency that comes to mind.

This is because you have imprinted your agency's brand onto your audience's long-term memory and you've added credibility when no one else has.

That means you won't have to bend over backward for leads entering the buy phase because they'll already be interested in you. Plus, if you already have them in your database, then you don't have to pay for expensive media buying over and over to keep your agency growing.

So, how do you reach the part of your audience who isn't looking for you?

In order to get in front of the 4% in the research phase and the 92% who aren't even looking, you can conduct community outreach programs, give back to the community (online or offline) or diversify your lead sources.

Just remember, the more of those businesses you can get in front of now, the faster your agency will be positioned for explosive growth. **So get after those leads!**

Step 3: Lead Generation Framework

There are three primary components to getting a flood of consistent leads for your agency. Without all three components in place, tested, and proven you'll continue to struggle with the peaks and valleys of lead flow that strangle your agency's growth potential. But getting these three components in place and working together will catapult your agency to the next level!

The keyword is together.

All three components go hand-in-hand; their success is dependent upon each other, so the trick is finding the winning combination

The Three Primary Components For Lead Flow:

1. Lead Magnets – A lead magnet is a creative way to incentivize your target audience into providing basic contact information. Generally, this means providing a free PDF, e-book, free trial, etc. Customize your lead magnet to appeal to your target audience.

2. Calls To Action – This is typically the actual button, form, or tagline that spurs a prospect to take action, for example, "Click Here" or "Call Now." This prompts the customer to get the lead magnet so that you get their information.

3. Traffic Generation – This can come from a variety of sources, this is something you should test constantly to make sure you are getting high-quality traffic from your traffic generation sources. Not all traffic is created equally, I would prefer to have 100 site visits from my target audiences and land 10 projects than receive 1000 site visits and land 5 projects. Make sure to check out our Traffic Generation course for more information on how to drive targeted traffic to your digital assets.

Again, the sales pipeline is an integral part of your agency's lead-harvesting success. Having a sales pipeline will ensure that all of those calls to action, lead magnets, and traffic generation efforts aren't wasted. It will make sure that all leads are followed up with until they "buy or die." Indefinite follow-up will allow your agency to do more with less, meaning close more of the leads you already have.

Don't make the mistake of not having diverse calls to action on your websites or digital assets. What I mean by "diversifying" your calls to action is essentially this: having a "contact us" form is not enough even if they really want to work with your agency. You've got to put yourself in front of them and make it as easy as possible to reach you.

Now, **there is such a thing as overdoing it.** I suggest using 5 or 6 different types of calls to action throughout all of your digital assets (website, landing pages, social media pages, etc.). This way you'll appeal to a wider variety people, and if someone visits several of your assets they won't be bombarded with the same prompt over and over again.

Even though I have found 5 or 6 to be a good average, at the end of the day the only thing that matters is what your target audience likes and engages with. This is why I highly recommend you implement a "Call to Action Conversion" grading system.

This grading system should allocate for conversion percentages, client types, traffic sources and total revenue generated by specific lead magnets and calls to action. **Below we provide the top 13 converting calls to action for digital assets.**

Having a small strip above the menu bar is a great way to catch prospects attention.

Have this slide in after they've been on the site for 10-15 seconds.

It's also a good idea to switch them up for page refreshes and revisits. You'll also want to have different ones for your individual digital assets.

People who visit your blog are probably researching your agency or a specific topic, so you should provide a research-based lead magnet.

The Top 13 Converting Calls To Action

1. **Header** - the header image is the first thing people see when they visit your website. If you're running a special or have a featured program/package/service you should create a banner image that entices them to learn more, get the free trial, and so on.

2. **Menu** - in the menu you can place an animated gif or different colored button to capture your target audience's attention and get them to click on something specific. Again, this could take them to a free trial, free download, etc.

3. **Slider** - there are several options for sliders: top of page, footer, chat, and header. They can be set up to provide movement every 10-15 seconds while on your page. It's a good idea to coordinate all of these to capture your target audience's attention span as often

as possible, without being annoying. Make them unique. You wouldn't need more than two of these per pages

4. **Footer** - Footer is a simple strip that appears at the bottom of the page. You can either have it static or on a timer. If it's on a timer, coordinate it with other timed elements on the page.

5. **Messenger** - Facebook messenger is great because they can opt into your list at one single click of a button, no forms required! Have a button on your page that links to Facebook messenger, or include it on your contact us page. When people send you a message via the messenger app, you'll be "connected" and have the ability to send them push notifications.

6. **Chat** - every day this call to action delivers better and better results. More and more people hate getting on the phone, so chat is a great alternative. You don't want to miss out on answering a question or clarifying something for a prospect just because they weren't ready to get on the phone. Chat allows them to hide behind the digital wall until they're ready to take it to the next level.

7. **Exit** - considering how many people "hate" exit pop-ups, you'd think they wouldn't work, but they are actually incredibly effective! Exit pop-ups outperform

all other calls to action by at least 2-to-1 and in most cases 3-to-1. People hate them because they stop or interrupt them, but they engage with them because they stop and interrupt them. If you're not interrupting your prospects, they may never slow down enough to notice you.

8. **Resources/assets/services page** - on your resources, assets, or services page you should have numerous different types of free content or free consult calls to action. If prospects make it to one of these pages they're almost generally looking for something specific. So, make sure you give them specific options that suit their needs.

9. **Video** - in your videos you should give a specific call to action for your prospects to take action. If you're using YouTube or other popular video hosting platforms, you can usually have the call to action appear in the video at a predetermined time interval. Something like "click here for your free download" or "click below to subscribe."

10. **Contact us page** - it sounds simple, but it's still one of the highest converting calls to action. This is because when people specifically seek you out, the first thing they look for is your contact us page. So if your brand positioning vortex is pulling prospects in as it should be, your contact us page becomes increasingly

important.

11. **Phone number** - this seems obvious, right? Always have your phone number on your website and make sure that it's a hyperlink so that they can click on it to call you. More and more people are searching on mobile devices so make calling you as easy as possible, especially since a phone call is the #1 opportunity to sell or upsell.

12. **On demand appointment** - on-demand scheduling is becoming more and more prevalent, but it's still not on every website, email and digital asset out there. If you don't have an on-demand meeting scheduling platform set up already, you need to right away. And then you should plaster it everywhere on your site and within every email you send. It saves your prospects' time as well as your own and gives your prospects another avenue to reach out to you.

13. **Social media connect** - all websites should allow your prospects to connect with you on social media. Remember, it's about connecting with your target audience in a format they're familiar with. Also, it's a bonus if it's a social media platform they use on a daily basis!

TIP: You can't just pick your personal favorite social media platform. If your favorite platform is Facebook, and you're incredibly present on Facebook, but your target audience's favorite platform is Instagram, you're wasting your time and efforts AND you're missing out on a great opportunity on Instagram.

MAP MARKER

Please don't make the rookie mistake of thinking that a small, subtle call to action will work.

I hear this more and more: "If they really like my agency or want me bad enough, they'll seek me out on their own." This makes me cringe. The truth is: they do want your agency, but they're ridiculously busy and need a little motivation.

It's your job to give them every opportunity to work with your agency and make it as easy as possible for them to get in touch with you by having numerous calls to action throughout your digital assets. Also, different prospects have different pain points, so give them different free content options, scheduling options, etc

Not all lead magnets are created equal, so what makes a great lead magnet? What makes some lead magnets convert and others fail? Make sure your lead magnets follow these 6 rules, and your lead magnets should be world class.

1. Quick and easy to digest – your lead magnet shouldn't take more than 10 minutes to read, watch, or consume. It should deliver overwhelming value but make your prospects want to come back for more: the following upsell in your client path.

2. Targets a specific problem – it should laser focus on one specific problem that your target audience has, then it should show them how to solve that problem. By solving just one problem, even if it's small, you'll leave a positive impression in the mind of the lead. Don't be too vague in efforts to "not give too much away." Be generous with your information if you really want them to trust you.

3. Provides a quick win – if you can't solve the whole problem, it should at least deliver a quick win. Not all problems are solvable in less than under 10 minutes, but make sure the lead experiences some form of success or satisfaction and associates that with your agency's brand.

4. Delivers overwhelming value – even though it's free, it has to deliver overwhelming value. Your prospects will judge the quality of your agency based upon the quality of the lead magnet, so you need to wow them. Again, be generous with info. 5. Instantly accessible – don't make them wait or you'll lose them! Give them instant access via email or instant download from your website. If it isn't available in 60 seconds or less, they may forget about you or grow impatient and lose interest.

6. Increases brand positioning – the lead magnet should build value in your agency's brand positioning. Don't position yourself as stingy, or as cheap, or as a quick fix. This is your chance to position your agency as a talented expert in your field.

As with most suggestions we give you, not 100% of these lead magnets will work for your agency. Through split testing and tracking you can figure out which ones work the best for you specifically and appeal most to your target audience. Our Lead Magnet Creation worksheet will help you with this process. You'll pick a lead magnet; give it a catchy title, and check to see if it meets the criteria to be world class.

Here are the Top 12 Lead Magnets for you to choose from:

1. Free report – provide an industry or community related report that is relative to your specific niche, community or location. Reports can be lengthy and should contain detailed information about its topic.

2. Free guide/cheat sheet/handout – produce an informative study guide, cheat sheet or handout for your target audience. These are more interactive than reports. They should contain more "do it yourself" sections.

3. Free tool kit – "tools" are customizable documents or spreadsheets templates that your prospects can edit and use for cc themselves. Something that makes your prospects' lives a little bit easier and takes a little work off of their plate.

4. Free micro course – produce a free "micro course" if you have membership capabilities on your website. These courses are a bit of an undertaking but convert well because they include a ton of freebies in one place: short lecture videos, interactive workbooks, and a few basic tools or templates.

5. Free trial – if you offer software with your agency, figure out a way to give prospects a free trial. This might not apply to you – but if it does, this is a great giveaway.

6. Free e-book/book – this magnet been around forever but is still very effective

7. Free quiz/survey/assessment – create a quiz, survey, or assessment tool that is fun, creative, and provides high value. Let them go through the entire process and then offer to send them the final report via email. Get creative with this because it's a great opportunity to get information and insight on your leads.

8. Free consult – most prospects that use this lead magnet are ready to take action and are in the buy or research phase, meaning they're very hot leads. You'll also find that the people who engage are much more serious simply because they're willing to get on the phone, which requires them to give up personal time.

9. Free webinar – a weekly or monthly webinar is always a good idea. The odds are you won't have hundreds of people beating down the registration page but the prospects that do show up will be very hot.

10. Free templates – if you have a useful tool in a template form, put it as a free giveaway on your digital assets. Templates are made to save people time and make life easier, so you're automatically providing a quick win.

11. Monthly newsletter – everyone who gives you their email address should be in your monthly newsletter. This is a prime opportunity to position your brand, inform your prospects about your services, and deliver overwhelming value. Don't just throw together a newsletter. Make sure it's interesting, relevant, engaging, and informative.

12. Case studies – provide client related case studies for your prospects. This way they can read about your prior successes. If it's possible try to get a third party to write the case study it builds more value and seems more credible if it comes from someone

Step 4: Best Management Practices For Lead Magnets

Eliminate Competition: Use your lead magnets to create doubt in your competitor's services or brand by asking creative questions. Go the extra mile beyond whatever your competitors are offering. Don't be like everyone else selling what you sell.

Bring The Pain: and get on your prospect's level instead of following the crowd and doing exactly what your competition does. Be innovative and creative, give away more for free than your competitor does. Be the best and obvious choice.

Test, Test, And Test Again!: You should always be testing your lead magnets. There is no such thing as having the perfect lead magnet or call to action. The industry changes every hour of every day, so you should constantly be striving to improve what you're putting in front of your prospects. If you see there's something new that's converting better than what you've always used, take the time to create that lead magnet and improve it – again, go the extra mile.

Make Them Fun: You can cover very serious topics and still have fun. Make it fun for your target audience. Your prospects will not click on something that looks boring and hard to consume. That want quick, easy, interesting, and fun. Of course, that doesn't mean sloppy or cheap. Find the perfect balance for your target audience – everyone's is totally different.

Thank You Pages – These are shown normally after a prospect opts in to one of your lead magnets, but it's one of the biggest indicators of engagement level. At my first agency, we knew if they completed the 'Thank You' page questions, they were a hot lead. So we got on the phone with them immediately and used the opportunity to upsell. If someone opts in to your lead magnet, have a 'Thank You' page to follow-up, and a sales pitch ready to go if they fill it out.

★ **MAP MARKER**
*Real World Meets Digital...Business Card Harvesting...*Most CRM (customer relationship management) applications come with the ability to take a photo of business cards and have them automatically dumped into your CRM.

Usually, it's an easy to use app on your phone, and many CRMs provide them for free now! If for some reason your CRM doesn't have this ability, it's your responsibility to make sure *every single* business card you get is put into your CRM platform, educated, and engaged by a sales rep or your personally, even if it is to just say hi.

Business cards can be a gold mine even if you rarely meet people in person.

Think about how I mentioned going to Jay Conrad Levinson's private events, I would learn so many amazing strategies and tactics it was mind blowing, but the best nuggets I got out of those events would be over dinner and drinks after the event was completed.

Well, you can bet I harvested some business cards from that event and every other event I attended; we were dedicated to data entering the contacts into our CRM with automated follow up processes.

After a few years of events, lunches, dinners, cruises and so on, we had a marketing database of well over 10,000 successful small business owners across the globe. As you can imagine that was critical to our ability to hit our sales goals month after month.

⭐ MAP MARKER

Activity Dashboards – Every CRM platform has different activity dashboards and reporting options. An activity dashboard allows you to watch people's actions in real time. In Infusionsoft this is called "Recent Activity" and it allows you to see when people are opening emails, clicking links, or filling out a contact us pages. Having someone monitor this activity dashboard is a GREAT way to harvest leads. If you see someone click your on-demand calendar link, but they don't actually schedule a meeting, then pick up the phone and call them. A lot of times the only reason they didn't book is that they got interrupted. Calling them shows initiative and opens up a conversation

Lead Harvesting Wrap Up

As you can see there's a lot that goes into lead harvesting.

Don't make the mistake of thinking that if you have more traffic you'll get more leads.

This is not the case, it's all about your ability to entice your target audience and capture their contact information, whether it is live events, Facebook Lives, Webinars, Your Website, and so on…

First, you must get your lead harvesting formula dialed in, and then you can focus on driving more traffic to your digital assets.

Traffic is one of the most expensive things you'll pay for, and if you don't have enticing lead magnets and calls to action you won't see a return.

I learned this one the hard way by paying for traffic until I got up to 3,000 visitors a month, but the number of leads didn't go up.

I was dumbfounded and downright mad. I learned the hard way that without a high converting lead harvesting strategy, all the traffic in the world is pointless.

Take the best management practices, call to action tactics, lead magnets and manual lead harvesting tips we provided in this chapter and get a strategy in place for your agency.

As always, if you ever have any questions, don't hesitate to give us a call. Always remember we're here to serve! Niche or local market - Never let a lead fall through the cracks, they should be put into an automated campaign and nurtured indefinitely.

Check out our Sales and Marketing Automation course for a detailed guide including mind maps on how to best nurture your prospects at every stop in the sales pipeline link is in the resources area.

MONTH SIX

The process of traffic generation has changed, and agency owners need to find new ways to reach quality interested buyers rather than spending tons of money for low quality worthless leads.

Chapter 6

Traffic Generation

You are about to learn how to pay for traffic wisely. We'll show you how to put your money where the quality leads are rather than spending tons of money on leads that will never have intention to buy from you. Also, you'll learn how to organically get high quality traffic.

Let me caution you on falling into the trap of thinking that more traffic equals more business for your agency. This is NOT the case.

When it comes to traffic, it's about quality over quantity. To ensure that you're getting the best traffic for the lowest price, there are a couple of things you must learn first. In this chapter, we're going to explain the P.O.P. framework, Guerrilla marketing warfare, the Top 30 traffic generation sources, the KPIs you need to evaluate those sources, and to wrap up, we will warn you of some common mistakes' agencies make as it pertains to Traffic Generation.

Armed with all of this knowledge, you'll be ready to create a traffic generation strategy for your agency and become a traffic generation master! Regardless of how you get traffic, all traffic generation follows our P.O.P. framework.

Ultimately, there are three different types of traffic your agency will need to have in its arsenal to create the explosive growth we all desire.

Three Types Of Traffic

1. PAY FOR IT NOW – Paying for traffic now is normally very expensive up front, but it's required to build a sustainable and fast-growing agency. This can range from Google Adwords, Facebook Ads, Sponsored Banner Ads, Tradeshow Events, etc. Paid traffic sources can also be turned on and off as you see fit, allowing you to control your service bandwidth.

2. ONGOING EFFORT – This is organic SEO, content syndication, social media content marketing, blogging, etc. Organic traffic generally requires a long-term strategy and it takes longer to build up a substantial organic traffic base. However, organic traffic historically converts at a higher rate and has a longer life cycle. A longer life cycle means that once you get a high-ranking blog article or domain name with high traffic keywords, it could generate traffic for months or even years until someone knocks you out of your position. This means it takes more time and effort to get in place, but the ROI for revenue and brand penetration is huge.

3. PAY FOR IT LATER – These are typically joint ventures, affiliates, referral partners or co-promotional events. In these cases, everyone is aware of the payout percentages and there is the ability to track all leads and sales. These relationships can take some time to establish but it works wonders for driving huge amounts of revenue to your agency. I'm a big fan of referral partner marketing. If you can establish 10-12 consistent referral partners that send you 1-3 projects a quarter your agency is poised for a massive explosion of growth.

There are pros and cons to all types of traffic. Eventually you will need to master all three mentioned in the POP framework, so you can grow and scale your agency to new heights. If you're a small agency just starting out, it's okay to have just one or two traffic sources for now, but eventually you'll need to graduate to numerous different traffic sources and have unique strategies for each.

If you're a more advanced and established agency, then you need to focus on setting up a closed loop sales and marketing system to track all aspects of your client path. Ultimately, it's up to you to decide what types of traffic generation best fit your agency

★ MAP MARKERS

Never forget that traffic is useless without a converting call to action. Make sure you go through our Lead Harvesting course to learn how to diversify and optimize your calls to action.

Traffic generation is like Guerrilla Warfare because every agency in your market or niche is trying to capture the same target audience, and you must fight to be the one that comes out on top. There are only so many leads looking for services at any given time, so you must act as if you're in full combat against your competitors, so your agency gets every lead. Only then will you prevail over your competition

GUERRILLA MARKETING IS DEFINED AS: Going after conventional goals using unconventional tactics.

My marketing mentor, Jay Conrad Levinson, created a list of 100 marketing weapons.

It's an exceptional list of creative ideas, but technology has come a long way since he wrote it. Also, not all of them were geared towards agencies like yours.

So, I pulled the best choices from that list and combined it with my 15 years of agency experience to produce the Top 30 Traffic Generation Sources specifically for digital marketing agencies.

The more of these you can get in place, the more successful your agency will be. Your prospects only have so many dollars to spend and they're only going to spend those dollars with one agency. It should be your mission to aggressively go after each and every one of those dollars.

Get creative, think outside the box, and remember: **this is warfare.**

Below is the key we will use to evaluate the Top 30 traffic generation sources.

Top 30 Traffic Generation Evaluation Key

PN	Pay for it Now (Money Spent to Get it Going Now)
OG	Ongoing Resources Required to Maintain
PL	Pay for it Later (Commissions or Partner Payouts)
OR	Organic Traffic Sources (Traffic Sources Using Labor)
PD	Paid (Media Buying) Traffic Sources
ROI	Time until you see a Return on Investment
COST	Cost projections

Cost projections

🅰 **VERY CHEAP**

🅰🅰 **CHEAP**

🅰🅰🅰 **MODERATELY PRICED**

🅰🅰🅰🅰 **EXPENSIVE**

🅰🅰🅰🅰🅰 **VERY EXPENSIVE**

Selecting which traffic generation sources to pull from can seem a bit overwhelming, but the descriptions and key below should help you find clarity.

As we've said before, the best options are dependent upon your agency's needs. It will take trial, error, and testing to discover exactly which sources will provide the best results.

Regardless of what source you pick, all traffic generation should be held to a standard of excellence and if they fall short they should be removed and replaced by another tactic.

This process should continue until you have at least 7 – 10 proven traffic generation sources for your agency to explode from.

Step 1: Learn To Drive Traffic By Paying Up Front

Facebook Groups – Get involved, stay involved, and if possible delegate the management of dozens of groups. Don't sell in these groups, you'll get kicked out and it's always better to give than receive. So, share freebies, information, or relevant content. Through the act of giving, you'll receive in abundance.

Key: PN, OG, OR, PD, ROI = Immediate and Long-Term, **Cost:**

Facebook Ads – This is one of the hottest options right now, so get on board or get left behind! There's an art form to running Facebook Ads, so either dive into learning the tricks or hire someone who already knows them. I highly suggest hiring an expert to get it set up for you unless of course, you are the expert.

Key: PN, PD, ROI = Immediate, **Cost:**

Facebook Remarketing Pixel – This is a must for anyone running ads via Facebook. If a prospect lands on your website, landing page, ad or Facebook page you can continue to deliver ads to them for up to 6 months. The ad delivery cost on this very cheap and gets amazing results.

Key: PN, PD, ROI = 15-30 days, **Cost:**

Facebook messenger – there are new apps and programs that allow you to send private messages via messenger. If a lead responds, then you're connected through the messenger app and you'll be able to send push notifications. Huge opportunity! You can also run messenger ads (driving them to your messenger for an opt-in), which is a very cool feature.

Key: PN, OG, OR, PD, ROI = Immediate and Long-Term, **Cost:**

Facebook organic – create a business page and constantly post relative content, invite prospects, clients, friends and anyone else you can think of to like your page. Stay consistent with this and I would highly suggest gamifying it as much as possible to get organic likes and comments.

Key: PN, OG, OR, ROI = 2-3 months, **Cost:**

Google Adwords – A little more expensive, but a good investment. The possibilities are endless on this platform and they keep adding new features that make it even more powerful. Be patient with this tool, it takes months to dial in the right keyword set, ad groups, ad copy, etc. Once you crack the code though, the phones will be ringing off the hook! The beauty of this paid media is that once you get it dialed in, you can turn on new business and turn it off like a water faucet. When you have the ability to do that, you're headed straight to the 8-figure arena!

Key: PN, PD, ROI = Immediate and Long-Term, **Cost:**

Google Remarketing – A must if you're paying for traffic or have a lot of organic traffic coming to your site. If anyone visits your site, you should keep your brand in front of them as often as possible.

Key: PN, PD, ROI = Immediate and Long-Term, **Cost:**

Sales Navigator – This is an advanced search tool provided by LinkedIn and it's amazing. You can really dial in your target audience with this tool and in most cases, you can even send private messages directly to the business owners. Figure out the Sales Navigator and you'll be amazed at the amount of data you can harvest. Then you can create a strategy around all of the data you harvested, like harvesting small business owners phone numbers and conducting an outbound call campaign to schedule meetings or to give them some free content to establish a relationship.

Key: PN, OG, ROI = 1-4 Weeks, **Cost:** (A)

Twitter – You can do a lot through Twitter. Advertising, content creation, increase your followers, engage with leads, etc. There are tons of opportunities, you just need to get familiar with the platform to utilize it to its fullest potential.

Key: PN, OG, OR, PD, ROI = Immediate for Paid Ads, 2-4 Months Organic, **Cost:**

Pinterest, Instagram, Snapchat, Etc. – This is just a few of the larger social media platforms, but if your target audience is on them than you can harvest leads from them! I would recommend sticking to the bigger platforms because you can get in front of more people.

Key: PN, OG, OR, PD, ROI = Immediate and Long-Term, **Cost:**

Direct Mail – A lot of "digital gurus" said that direct mail was dead 10 years ago, boy were they wrong. Direct mail is more effective than ever, it's also cheaper than ever. Now that our mailboxes aren't stuffed to the max with promotional items we get excited when we see something new. Since a lot of companies are diversifying their marketing efforts away from direct mail, it's a prime opportunity for you to get in front of your target audience where your competitors aren't.

Key: PN, PD, ROI = 1-2 Weeks from time of mailing, **Cost:**

Radio – If you're a local service provider, you really need to look into radio advertising. It's cheap and most of us still listen to the radio while we're in the car. When picking which radio station I recommend focusing on talk radio, it tends to convert at a higher rate and focuses more on specific target audiences. For example Business Talk Radio- This does not include podcasting or Internet Radio.

Key: PN, OG, or PD, ROI = Immediate and Long-Term, **Cost:**

Trade Shows – This is a requirement for all agencies. If you're local, sign up for the local business trade show, or go to the closest metro area and attend a small business educational seminar. The ability to meet people face-to-face is, and will always be, the highest converting method of driving revenue.

Key: PN, OG, or **PD,** ROI = Immediate and Long-Term, **Cost:**

Billboards/street Signs – This is another tactic most people never think of advertising with anymore, but they WORK, and they work big time. Billboards are a great way to reach the masses – to reach where they commute, live, work and they are even digitalized. This mainly applies to local digital agencies, but it's great for brand penetration.

Key: PN, OG, or **PD,** ROI = Immediate and Long-Term, **Cost:**

Outbound Call Campaigns – I have never seen an aggressive outbound call campaign that didn't work. Every agency in the world has a contact list of old clients and leads they can pick up the phone and call, just make sure you have a compelling reason on why you're calling. For example, "We're taking a survey of local business owners and would like to get your feedback, can we get your updated contact information, so we can send it or email it to you." By default there will be a small percentage that just so happens to be in the market for your services, this will get traffic in the door for as close to free as possible.

Key: PN, OG, OR, PD, ROI = Immediate and Long-Term, **Cost:**

Community Outreach – Become more active in your community, whether it's a national CRM community, precise industry niche or your local community. The more active you become in those communities the more people will recognize and know about you. This means you'll generate more traffic and it'll convert at a higher rate than cold traffic.

Key: PN, OG, OR, PD, ROI = Immediate and Long-Term, **Cost:**

Sponsorship – After defining your avatar or target audience, research and find sites, blogs, or physical locations they frequent. Reach out to these places and discuss sponsoring a blog post, email blast, podcast series, or live event.

Key: PN, OG, or PD, ROI = Immediate and Long-Term, **Cost:**

Client outreach – This is a simple campaign that gets you in front of your existing clients. To put this in perspective I'll share a story.

A local digital agency decided to deliver doughnuts to their clients one month. Every morning they would drop off a dozen doughnuts on the way to work.

The clients were very happy to get free doughnuts, so you improved your relationship with existing clients, but it also drove a ton of new business in the door. While in the office delivering the doughnuts a lot of the clients would strike up a conversation about another project they had been meaning to tackle.

So, while sharing a doughnut they would discuss it for a few minutes and then schedule a follow-up meeting. They spent less than $200 on the entire campaign and it generated thousands of dollars of new business from existing clients.

On top of driving a ton of revenue and improving a long-term relationship with the client, it led to a bunch of referrals. Who wouldn't tell their friends about the free donuts for a month! This is an example of Guerrilla Marketing at its finest.

Client outreach doesn't have to be this extensive, but make sure to reach out to them and do something to improve your relationship; it'll only help you in the long run.

Key: PN, OG, OR, PD, ROI = Immediate and Long-Term, **Cost:**

Directory marketing – The *Better Business Bureau, Digital Agency Network, Clutch.co*, and others are great resources to get traffic.
There may even be directories specific to your area or niche. They're usually paid and start to drive traffic immediately. They normally help with organic SEO as well.

Key: PN, OG, OR, PD, ROI = Immediate and Long-Term, **Cost:**

Ongoing Effort Traffic Sources

Google My Business And Maps – Sign up for the Google My Business program, it's free and will get you listed on Google Maps. This can be a huge ROI for your agency, and it gets you listed in numerous other apps like Waze, etc. It'll also allow you to create a large snapshot of your agency on the left-hand side of the organic search results, depending on how close your prospects are, you could be the only option there, again a huge opportunity for leads.

Key: OG, OR, ROI = 30 Days, **Cost:**

Search Engine Optimization – Organic SEO is one of the most powerful tools you have in your arsenal. It is a long-term strategy and takes persistence, but if you stick to it and have a keyword strategy behind the content you create, it can drive long-term and high converting traffic to your agency for years to come.

Key: OG, OR, ROI = 3-6 Months, **Cost:**

Linkedin – Research local businesses or businesses in your niche via the news feeds, syndicate content, and engage with them via traditional LinkedIn search functions. I also recommend looking into LinkedIn advertising opportunities.

Key: OG, OR, ROI = 1-4 Weeks, **Cost:**

Blog/Vlog – This is usually part of an organic SEO strategy, but regardless of how you use it, DO IT!!
This is a long-term strategy in most cases, but the more credibility your domain name gets as a result of syndicating blog content, the higher all of your pages will rank and the more traffic you will receive. If you have high quality and relevant content popping up in search engines leads will stumble upon you while they're researching and remember you when they're ready to buy.

Key: OG, OR, ROI = 4-6 Months, **Cost:**

Step 2: Learn To Build Your Passive Traffic Sources

TRAFFIC GENERATION

Podcast – Convert your vlogs into a podcast, interview local rock stars, community rock stars, etc.

Key: OG, OR, ROI = 1-6 Months, **Cost:**

Content Syndication – This will help improve organic SEO rankings and drive traffic from third-party sites. Reach out to websites who also serve your market/niche and allow guest content providers. Sign up to be a guest blogger or whatever it is they offer and write high value content for their sites.

Make sure you get backlinks to your site, this will help with your organic rankings and you'll get traffic from the content you provided on their website.

Key: OG, OR, PD, ROI = Immediate and Long-Term, **Cost:**

Email Marketing – This should be a no brainer and every agency in the world should already be doing this. To improve the effectiveness and increase efficiency you should take it to the next level and automate your entire sales and marketing process.

 See Sales and Marketing Automation course in the resources section

This is too powerful of a tool to not be utilizing. Set Up a MailChimp or Constant Contact account, harvest contact information from every single lead you come across and put them in your newsletter or drip email nurturing campaign.

Key: OG, OR, ROI = Immediate and Long-Term, **Cost:**

Marketing Automation – True marketing automation goes well beyond simply scheduling predefined emails to go out on specific dates at specific times. True marketing automation will allow you to automate voicemail messages, schedule follow-up task reminders, send texts, syndicate Facebook content, and just about anything you can dream up. Every dollar spent on setting up automated systems for your agency is a dollar well spent. Automation tools can and should work for your agency for years to come if done correctly.

Key: OG, OR, **PD**, ROI = Immediate and Long-Term, **Cost:**

Refer A Friend Program – I like to automate this, but regardless of how you do it you need to have a formal referral program in place. This is different than a referral partners a refer a friend program is typically a one-off type of lead. Ask clients at the end of their projects if they know of anyone else that needs your services. As long as you wowed them they should send you referrals that close higher than any other lead you will get. So make sure you give all friend referrals special attention and really think through the automation process.

Key: PL, **OG**, OR, **PD**, ROI = Immediate and Long-Term, **Cost:**

Joint Ventures – In the traditional agency space, joint ventures work, but not as well as referral partners. If you have an educational course or informational product, go the joint venture route. Proceed with caution when it comes to joint ventures though, a lot of JV companies don't care about your brand, they're only out for the EPC's (Earnings Per Click) and will do anything to get that number as high as possible, regardless of how it affects you.

Key: PL, ROI = 2-4 Weeks, **Cost:** (On Revenue Only)

Referral Partners – I am a HUGE fan of referral partners. These are long-term relationships that send you very hot leads on a consistent basis. They typically attach their brand with yours, so they care about how your brand performs and is represented. A successful referral partner relationship will mean you're both interested in each other's success. Think about companies that serve the same target audience, compile a list, pick up the phone, and start a dialogue. Make sure you have a plan ready to present before you get on the phone, as always if you need help creating that plan, let us know and we would be glad to serve your agency

Key: PL, ROI = 2 Weeks, **Cost:** (On Revenue Only)

I could literally list hundreds of possible traffic sources, but the few listed above are the ones I have found to get the best results for agencies like yours.

After reviewing the list above, you should pick the 5 traffic generation sources that best fit your agency and put together a road map on how you're going to implement them.

Step 3: Monitor Your Leads Through The Key Performance Indicators

You should never set up a traffic source and forget about it or assume that it's working simply because it worked in the past. Your agency should constantly monitor the results of all traffic generation campaigns.

There are 11 traffic generation KPIs you should always track.

The 9 below should be tracked and monitored for the first 6 months to see if a new traffic source is providing qualified leads and is worth the investment.

1. **MEDIA BUDGET AD SPEND** – Total amount of money spent on a traffic source.

2. **TOTAL VISITORS** – Traffic directly attributed to that particular source.

3. **BOUNCE RATES** – How many people from that traffic source left your digital asset (website, landing page, etc.) after visiting only one page.

4. **OPT INS** – Tracking opt-ins is easier when you have a specific landing page for paid traffic sources. Each one should be attributed back to the specific traffic source. Organic traffic isn't as easily tracked, but all efforts should be taken to determine where your leads were generated.

5. **LEAD TO CLOSE RATIO** – How long it takes to close a prospect into a paying client once they have opted in to your call to action.

6. **INITIAL INVESTMENT ROI** – Most projects will have more revenue generated in the first 90- 180 days of the project.

The amount of revenue generated in this time should be considered the Initial Investment ROI.

7. **CLIENT ACQUISITION COST** – How much it costs to acquire a new client.

8. **TOTAL COST OF PROJECT (6 MONTHS)** – When you start turning leads into clients, you need to measure how much it costs to effectively fulfill those new projects during the first 6 months.

9. **TOTAL PROJECT PROFIT (6 MONTHS)** – The new clients and new projects will be generating profits. You need to know which traffic sources the most profitable clients came from over the first six months. After the first 6 months, you'll have a good idea about whether or not the traffic source is effective. If you decide to stick with it, you need to track the following two items long term.

After the first 6 months, you'll have a good idea about whether or not the traffic source is effective. If you decide to stick with it, you need to track **the following two items** long term.

---

10. **CLIENT RETENTION RATIO** – How long the average client stays with your agency after they become a paying client.

11. **TOTAL CLIENT LIFE CYCLE VALUE** – How much revenue and overall value the average client generates throughout the course of their relationship with your agency. It's important to test each traffic source for at least 90 days - preferably 6 months - to determine whether or not it's a good fit for your agency.

Each of these should get a final grade or quality score.

In the tools and resources section of this book, we included a link to where to gain access to a spreadsheet where you can plug your KPI data in and get the analysis you need.

Make sure you find out how to download that and monitor your KPIs. As you track these over time, it'll paint a clear picture of exactly what traffic generation sources generated the highest ROI for your agency. In the tools and resources section of this course, you'll notice a Traffic Generation KPI spreadsheet containing items similar to the ones below. This spreadsheet will be customizable specifically for your agency's use.

Top 10 Traffic Generation Mistakes

Traffic generation can be one of your biggest expenses and if you're doing it can be one of your best investments. Now, if you're NOT doing it correctly then it can be money thrown out the window with no hopes of an ROI. Obviously, you want to avoid losing money at all costs, every penny counts after all. With that in mind, we've compiled the top 10 mistakes an agency can make in its traffic generation efforts. Knowing about these mistakes means you can take all of the necessary precautions to avoid them

---

Pay close attention. These can make or break your agency.

---

1. **NO CLEAR GOALS** – Every traffic source should have a goal. If you cannot set a goal and measure its performance then don't spend your time or money on it, regardless of how good of a deal it is. Everything must be measured and quantified to ensure that it's helping you reach your goals and ROI.

2. **NO DEFINED TARGET AUDIENCE**– If you attempt to pay for traffic to attract a broad audience like "Small Business Owners" you WILL go bankrupt. First off, everybody is targeting them, second off your message will be splintered. This means by trying to reach everybody, you'll reach nobody. Make sure you know exactly who you're going after, this will make it easier to find them and easier to appeal to them.

3. **NOT SPLIT TESTING** – Before you spend any substantial advertising dollars, you should know for certain that your offer and landing page will convert well. This requires you to set up a landing page, drive a small amount of traffic to it, and split test it until you are certain that your offer is appealing to your target audience. This is a little more work up front but will save you a ton of money in the long run.

4. **IGNORING MOBILE** – Don't go to market unless you've optimized your content for mobile devices. The majority of your audience will consume your calls to action on their phones or tablets, so make sure it's easy to read and navigate on all devices.

5. **UNCLEAR KPIs** – **KPIs** will provide clarity on how well traffic generation sources are performing, they can also help track the progress of your bigger goals. Utilize our spreadsheet and stay on top of these numbers.

6. **FAILING TO CATER TO YOUR TARGET AUDIENCE** – Your target audience could care less about what about what

you think; they only care about what's in it for them. Never forget this. If you focus on giving your target audience what they want, when they want it, your traffic generation strategies will be very successful. Once you have them hooked you can gently guide them down your client path, but you've to reach them and get through to them first.

7. **TRYING TO BE A JACK-OF-ALL-TRADES** – Don't try to be everywhere, you'll wear yourself and your wallet out. Pick the 5-7 traffic generation platforms you want to focus your efforts on and focus on them until they have proven to be profitable or proven to be crap. Then you can add a couple more to the mix.

8. **BEING IMPATIENT** – Just when you think no one gives a damn about your content your target audience will start to actually take notice. So be patient and give it time. You have seen the call to action a thousand times, but your target audience is just now starting to notice it.

9. **BEING UNENGAGING** – Give your audience a reason to follow you. Be engaging and enticing to your target audience. You need to earn their trust, and being engaging and informative right off the bat will help win them over and leave a positive impression.

10. **FORGETTING TO FOLLOW UP** – Traffic generation is extremely time consuming and expensive, so you must MAXIMIZE every single opt-in that you get. Never take any of

them for granted, you should have a strategic plan for how you're going to follow-up with and close every single lead.

Traffic Generation Wrap Up

As you can see, traffic generation is one of the hardest pieces to building a sustainable agency. It's also arguably the most critical piece.

I learned this lesson the hard way, but it's always better to have more leads than you can handle.

That puts your agency in the driver's seat as it pertains to pricing, positioning, growth, scalability, venture capital investors, potential buyers.... basically everything. If you can control and predict the amount of traffic and leads your agency receives every single month, you can grow your agency as big or as boutique as you would like.

You can service 5000 clients a year and average $100 an hour, or you can service 50 clients a year and average $300 an hour.

But the best part is, that choice is <u>not</u> made for you. You become in control of your own success when you get your traffic generation strategy dialed in.

Each one of the traffic sources mentioned in this workbook (and any others for that matter) requires a unique and specific strategy with impeccably exact execution to be successful.

This is why I suggest picking a few to get started with and work until you either crush it, or you find out it's not a good fit for your agency.

Once you crack the code or determine it's no good, move on to the next round, and keep going until you have at least 7-10 world class, A+ traffic sources to sustain and build your agency around.

Don't forget that we are always here to serve. If you have any questions, don't hesitate to call or shoot us an email and we'd be happy to set aside some time for a quick meeting.

MONTH SEVEN

The chapter ahead is about managing an agency while slowly removing yourself it, however by setting a strong foundation of leadership using these techniques will give you and your agency a strong chance for success!

Chapter 7

Leadership

Your agency is your life! So how do you take your agency from where you are now to a place where it's agile, independent from you, and growing? To be the leader of a cutting-edge agency you must be flexible and adaptive, even at a moment's notice. You need to loosen the reins and allow your employees the freedom to make decisions and come up with solutions on their own. This chapter will teach you how to do just that!

Step 1: Learning The Basics

For your agency to grow and thrive without being tethered to you it needs a solid foundation to stand on. And that foundation starts with leadership.

The leadership framework you're about to learn was developed over years of trial and error at my first agency. Once we dialed it in we won top company culture awards, got nominations for elite business of the year, and my agency's growth took off. So, it's easy to say that what you're about to learn is without a doubt the most important piece of growing and scaling a successful agency. And we made it easy for you by breaking down agile agency leadership into 5 components.

5 Components of Leadership

The first component is Core Values. These act as the moral compass for your agency.

The second is Purpose Statement. Your agency's purpose statement acts as the north star, always guiding you in the right direction, but it isn't physically attainable.

The third component is your Mission Statement. This is your agency's plant the flag moment, your Mount Everest that propels your agency to new heights.

The fourth piece is Tribe Alignment. This component is more important for agencies than it is for most other businesses.

With our unbelievably smart and younger workforce it's critical to have the entire tribe in alignment with your vision. **The last component is Visualization.** This is the physical manifestation of your purpose statement throughout your office and agency culture.

We'll cover all of these in more detail and give you the tools you need to help your agency succeed.

*There is a link to access to a downloadable workbook in the resource area. If you have it...grab a drink and set aside some time to learn the ins-and-outs of agile agency leadership.

Step 2: Value Driven Core

Core values are a set of beliefs that permeate all aspects of your agency. They'll filter every single decision and will provide guidance for your employees every day at your agency and in their personal lives.

If you're thinking, why do I care about how they make decisions in their personal lives?

Well, every person has their own moral code, and you want to find the individuals whose beliefs are in alignment with your agency.

When you get a team of highly skilled and morally sound people all working together, the possibilities are endless there is a reason this is number one.

The core values are the "Soul" of your agency, they'll guide you through the good times, bad times, big decisions, and small decisions. They come from inside of YOU because as the leader of your agency you imprint your personal beliefs and values throughout all aspects of your agency, especially your employees.

So, they must be authentic, come from within, and be something you live by every day.

Your core values aren't a goal you set; they're who you already are and what you believe in. They'll stand the test of time and should be as relevant in 100 years as they are today. **Everybody in your agency should know the core values.**

Try creating an acronym around them or sing a song about them every day--whatever it takes make sure every employee understands them and aligns with them.

This is so important because if they can't remember them off the top of their head then they're not filtering all of their decisions through them and they're jeopardizing your agency's success and reputation.

 MAP MARKER – if you ever find yourself compromising one of your core values in any decision you make, it will come back to haunt your agency. Do <u>not</u> go through with any decision if it breaks even one of your core values.

Don't be frustrated if you get stumped when you're first trying to uncover your core values, it can be difficult to get started but it'll eventually identify a few clear and fundamental characteristics

The core values you choose should be able to provide your ideal moral character completely, but we recommend it doesn't become a long list. you should be able to define it in less than eight individual values, which should be plenty enough. There are only seven deadly sins after all.

Each of the values on your list should be concise as well, something you can easily recite in your head. brevity is your ally when helping you and your employees remember the significance these hold for your business.

Spend some time committed to discovering what core values you want to conduct your business by. Then, when you know what you believe set aside some time to really discuss with your partners and employees what you need from them. Discuss with them and find what ways you could help them all remember and internalize this powerful framework for leadership.

Step 3: A Clear Purpose

Now that you've scheduled a time to meet with your trusted

team members about your core values it's time to go through the process of creating your agency's purpose statement.

Your purpose statement will act as the North Star for your agency and it defines your "Why". For example, the clothing brand --Life is Good's purpose statement is "Spreading the power of optimism." There is no end, no grand finale, but it offers constant inspiration.

Let's drive into creating your agency's purpose statement.

A purpose statement is intended to guide you as you constantly move forward but can never be physically achieved because it serves a higher purpose for your agency. Milestones, goals, ups, and downs will all come and go, but your purpose or the "why" you're in business will remain the same.

As your agency reaches different levels of greatness entirely new challenges will arise and your purpose statement will help guide you through all of it. A great purpose statement is broad, fundamental, inspiring, enduring and as I said in the core values module, it's to the point and around eight words long.

Now if you can't get it that short don't worry, it's more important that it conveys the true essence of why you're in business.
When creating your purpose statement, make sure you don't simply state what you do, there's nothing inspiring about that!

To help you get a great purpose statement in place there's a process that Jim Collins uses.

I don't normally use other coaches' work but honestly, the process he created 15 years ago is the best and most effective one I've ever seen. So, I'd like to give him and the Infusionsoft leadership team full credit for teaching and inspiring me, thanks to their guidance I was able to learn about a leadership framework and adapt it specifically for agencies. In the workbook and in chapter 2 of Beyond Entrepreneurship you'll find an outline of a process called the 5 Whys. The 5 Whys isn't a specific set of questions, it's more of a process that allows you to ask the 5 questions that are important to your agency.

Sometimes it's the same question repeated 5 times.

The point is to consistently ask yourself "why". Is what you wrote down important? Once you go through the exercise you'll learn whether or not you're going in the right direction. It's not uncommon to go through the process several times until you find a purpose statement that stands up to the scrutiny of the 5 Whys. Remember this isn't a race. When you ask "Why" 5 times it's important to be honest and really think about it. Research each word for synonyms, look up the meanings, and make every word count. when you're done with that move onto the next module where we'll cover how to create a mission statement for your agency.

Step 4: A Clear Mission

Up until this point we've been working on discovering the deeper meaning behind your agency. In this module we're going to set tangible goals. And not just any goal, but goals that when people first hear them they should think, is this person crazy? Your mission statement should be a big, hairy, audacious goal.

Let's drive in!

When everyone responsible for accomplishing your agency's mission first hears it, there should be a feeling of disbelief. Almost to the point of thinking it's impossible and you're crazy for even thinking that it could be accomplished in a 3 to 5 year time frame. When you get that reaction, smile! Because that's exactly what's supposed to happen when you establish your mission statement or as Jim Collins called it, your Big Hairy Audacious Goal. (BHAG)

There should only be a 50-70% chance of successfully hitting your goal. The point of having a BHAG is to inspire and encourage everyone to do things they previously thought were impossible. It's supposed to set measurable milestones of achievement that propel everyone toward greatness. If you want your agency to achieve greatness you can't aim for average, you have to aim higher than you ever thought possible.

A BHAG will help steer everyone in your agency in the same direction, and in order to reach it everyone will have to take their personal achievement levels up a few notches. When people start doing that something special happens, your staff will start to find creative new ways to accomplish old tasks, they'll get to work a little early and stay a little late. Not because you're forcing them to but because they want to achieve the group's mission and they don't want to let their peers down.

Change begins at the end of your comfort zone and for your agency to break through the 7 or 8 figure mark, everyone must change and strive for greatness as a unified entity.

To accomplish your BHAG you must have a defined path with measurable milestones. Set these milestones on an annual basis then break them down into monthly goals and hold people accountable for them.

Every person must hit their individual monthly milestones to achieve the ultimate goal, or what we like to call a "Plant the flag Moment" in your agency's history.

There are 4 types of mission statements but we're going to tell you the three that apply to agencies.

The first type of mission statement is **Targeting**.

Around our office we call this the "Red Dot" type of mission. So, once you set your sights on something, don't take your focus off of it until you've conquered your target. This mission can manifest itself in countless ways. Such as the number of businesses you've another target could be to change how an industry operates. I didn't know it at the time, but this was my mission when I started my first agency.

At the time the industry was in such demand it was filled with unethical digital service providers, including the one I worked for. It pissed me off so much that I decided to do something about it and I became hell bent on bringing a new level of ethics, integrity, and respect for the small business owners in the digital marketing industry. And I did it! Changed, "We will change 500 business owners' lives by the end of 2020."

The second type of mission statement is **the Common Enemy.**

This can apply to an agency in your niche or local market that's top dog and your mission can be to dethrone them.

We use this one at Digital Business Architects and it motivates all of us to strive for excellence and deliver only world class coaching solutions to our agency clients.

The third type of mission statement is the **"Role Model"**.

Think of a larger agency that you look up to and aspire to be like them one day. Pay attention to their decisions, branding, follow ups, culture, and all aspects of how they run their businesses.

Take what you learn, apply it to your agency, and then bring it to another level so can transition from a role model mission statement into a targeting mission statement.

Go Big or Go Home Right!

Step 5: Organize The Team

This step is aligning the tribe. The days of executives figuring out the vision for a company and telling everyone what they believe in are DEAD. That is the old fashion way to set up a leadership structure and the truth is that model NEVER worked for agencies!

Now, the workforce is much younger, smarter, and they have a deep need to understand the bigger picture. They have to know "Why" they're working for an agency or even working on a project.

At first this seem a little frustrating but once you understand it it's a powerful tool for motivation and powerful things can happen.

When you step back and think about it small businesses have always worked for a higher purpose.

They care about their employees, their employees' families, their life goals, and they want everyone involved to achieve happiness.

So, when you, as the agency owner, can get 3 – 40 people perfectly in alignment with your agency's vision the results are explosive

Let's drive into how to create that type of alignment…

The core of tribe alignment or group buy-in is the ability for the agency owner to accept the fact that they can't build a 7 or 8 figure agency by themselves.

You must humble yourself and understand that you can't do everything and be everywhere all of the time, therefore you must have help from employees. You must also trust and have faith that your employees are getting everything done in accordance with the core values, purpose, and mission.

Once that's done you schedule an agency wide meeting. It's best to have this meeting off site so people aren't distracted by phone calls, clients, or emails.

You need to frame this meeting under the context that everyone in the room will define the future of the agency. Everyone in the room will need to give feedback and be engaged in the process.

At the meeting start with defining the core values and explain how you came up with the ones you got.

It's normal for people to be unengaged at first but keep pushing them to get involved by asking questions, looking for input, and having them research and define words. Find creative ways to get everyone involved in the process.

Everyone being part of the process will help transfer an aspect of ownership to each and every employee. If they have input that changes one word in your agency's vision statement, they'll adopt it as their own. Once they adopt it as their own their dedication to your agency's performance will sky rocket. They'll start to give advice on how things should run, how to improve productivity, share creative ideas for team building events, and much more.

MAP MARKER

 There are so many benefits to implementing a tribe alignment leadership philosophy, but the best part is the confidence it gives you in knowing your agency can handle explosive growth without having quality assurance or refund issues. Your employees will take ownership in the agency and will take pride in making sure every single client is happy, without having to get you involved!

After you've completed the core values, move onto the purpose statement and finally work on the mission statement. Then we'll move on to how you can physically manifest the vision in your day-to-day office activities.

Step 6: Realizing The Vision

Now that you've discovered your agency's deeper meaning and gotten your tribe in alignment it's time to bring your vision to life In this step, we're going to cover how to physically manifest your vision throughout your office, lives, and culture

When something is physically represented around you in your daily activities it can have a major impact on your subconscious.

It becomes part of your language, activities, and guides you in all aspects of decision making. Visualization is how tribes achieve greatness.

Visualizing your mission statement, core values, and purpose statement throughout your office is something you should have a ton of fun with.

In my first agency the leadership team planned to let everyone off early on the Friday we had our tribe alignment meeting.

The employees didn't know that we had been planning this for months! When they left we brought in new furniture, wall decals, chairs, painted the walls, hung up whiteboards, and tons of other things. We redecorated the entire office to visually represent the "New" agency.

When the employees arrived the following Monday a member of the leadership team would give them a tour of the new offices and show them to their new desk.

It got the point across that we were a new agency as a result of everyone buying into the vision.

We were living the new vision and we were going to achieve greatness as a tribe.
The impact was staggering, over time employees that didn't live up to the core values were weeded out, and those that made it governed themselves and held the entire agency to a higher standard. That pride bled into every aspect of their work and eventually transformed the agency into a powerhouse.

The possibilities for visualization are endless!

We went on to add KPI cups, cornhole boards, vinyl pictures of team building events, we went white water rafting, had kickball tournaments, did wilderness survival training, and had family style cookouts that bonded the entire team. This turned the group into something bigger than just employees.

They were a tribe and as a unified tribe there was nothing that would stand in the way of achieving our mission!

Create fun contest, like quarterly T-Shirt contest, funniest Halloween costume, whatever you can think of! Have fun with this and get your employees engaged. It's all part of creating a tribe or family mentality built around accomplishing your agency's mission while adhering strictly to your agency's core values.

Visualization doesn't stop there though as the leader of your agency you must provide a vision of how your agency will look in the future.
A great example of this is an organizational chart. Have one that represents the agency as it is now and one that represents the agency when you achieve your mission.

It should show new positions that everyone can strive to achieve. This gives everyone something to work towards and next thing you know you'll have people asking you how they can be considered for the Vice President role on the future organizational chart.

Pay attention to these requests, there's a good chance they'll end up being your future vice president. Remember, if you can visualize it you can make it a reality.

Brainstorm a few new fun visualization tactics that you can implement to inspire your employees. When you're done you'll be ready to move on the next and final step!

Step 7: Bringing It All Back

Throughout the agile agency leadership course we've attempted to simplify a very complex issue. Most people will spend a decade and hundreds of thousands of dollars learning the tips and tricks we just gave you.

Don't underestimate the power of agile agency leadership. Even though we made it sound simple it's a critical step in building an award-winning agency culture. This is only the tip of the iceberg. Your success at becoming a better leader and developing the ability to inspire the people around you will determine how much you work and how much you make. And when we say "Make" around here, we mean profit AND time.

Leadership Wrap Up

Get the items in this course implemented, get your tribe in alignment, and watch the overwhelming impact it'll have on your agency.

Don't cut corners, with a few simple tweaks and brainstorming sessions you can have a leadership framework in place that will lay the foundation for explosive growth.

This topic can seem a bit overwhelming to navigate because the possibilities are endless, and it all comes down to YOU

MONTH EIGHT

As agency owners, we position ourselves to streamline and drive our teams by breaking up projects into accomplishable tasks. You are about to venture into one of the most important chapters of this book, because project management is vital, as it ensures there's a proper plan for executing on strategic goals.

Chapter 8

Project Management

Learn how to manage your projects in such a way that helps kill scope creep, keeps your clients happy and WOW'd by your services and staff, and yet still makes life easier on you and your team.

Introduction To Management

As I am sure you already know, there are thousands of moving parts to managing a digital marketing project. Managing a digital project creates a unique set of problems that offline projects do not encounter.

For example, expectation levels are extremely difficult to define. With virtual products, the client cannot physically hold or walk through it with you. If you build a house, the client can physically walk through the house, touch the countertops.

There's a "WOW" moment when you deliver a new house to a client. With a digital asset, there's nothing to physically walk through or touch. And what's worse, for people who aren't familiar with the virtual world, they perceive everything digital to be easy, so they ask for outrageous things that would never be asked for in the physical project management world.

Can you imagine a client demanding a homebuilder to build a mansion when they asked for and budgeted for a 3-bedroom ranch?

The client would look and feel like a total idiot!

But for some reason when dealing in the virtual world, they have no problem asking for outrageous items that seem "easy" to them.

In the same way you can't expect a homeowner to build a mansion with a ranch budget. Clients can't expect us to build Facebook when they have a budget for a simple website. This is just one example; there are hundreds of times something like this happened in my agency.

This one aspect of managing digital projects makes the "why" and the "how" you manage digital projects critical to the success of your agency. The project manager is ultimately responsible for profitability and productivity within the project, as well as creating raving fans.

You must have a strict project management process that ensures proper sign-offs from the client, strict guidelines for the project managers to follow, and knowing when to escalate to management or present change orders if something happens outside of those guidelines.

All of these can be moments in a project lifecycle that cause major problems and can cause you to either lose clients or go out of business.

Neither of which are positive for your agency or your quality of life.

Before we get started, you need to know that the overarching, most important, king of all philosophies of the project management of digital projects is:

The Importance Of Transparency

This seems so simple, but in reality, it is remarkably difficult to implement throughout your agency. It requires the ability to understand that a little pain now is better than a lot of pain later. It requires a strict adherence to using a cloud-based project management platform and the understanding that if anyone ever communicates outside of this platform, then it (in theory) did not actually happen and no action will be taken towards it.

It requires that you never skip a step we outline later in this chapter; in other words, **you can't go into the design phase without having the copy approved in writing first.**

Again, all of these things might sound simple, but when you start to tell clients (who are screaming at you) that you will not move forward until they use the project management platform, or they cannot get any programming done until the copy and the design concepts are approved in writing, you will figure out this is a lot harder than it sounds at first glance.

A few other things you need to have in place before we get started:

Project management methodology, Legal agreements that govern all aspects of the projects, Process management templates, and A strict process that all projects are required to follow.

We will go through all of these and the 8 steps of the perfect project management life cycle in this workbook. Let's get started by defining your project management methodology and communication standards.

Methodology

There are tons of project management styles out there, but in my opinion the best option for digital agencies is a hybrid between traditional project management systems (where everything is documented in great detail before anything begins) and a "scrum" version of the agile project management framework.

I normally like to give a few different directions, so you can choose which is best for your agency, but in this case this unique hybrid mix is absolutely custom tailored for effective project management in the digital agency industry.

MAP MARKER

I have found a lot of the things that are successful in the digital world turn out to be a healthy blend of the old school and new school methodologies or tactics. Use this to your advantage, do not try only "new school" tactics; remember the old school businesses were working just fine before the digital age.

The Agile/Scrum methodology is typically defined as having very little documentation up front and leaving it up to the teams to figure it out as they go. Though, most people seem to have many different opinions of what this means to them.

Regardless, this is a very important distinction to be made, because you no doubt have to leave a lot of freedom in the process for the teams to make decisions as they go through the process of creating world class websites, Facebook Ads, and so on.

The "hybrid" part of my system requires you to have a good amount of up front documentation before you get started. Keep in mind that Agile/Scrum was created for software development. Although (in most agencies) a programming component to your projects exists, it is not as intensive as a true software or application creation.

Normally it is more of a custom configuration of a CMS, or implementing custom CRM capabilities to get certain aspects of the project completed in accordance to the client's request. These are substantially easier to get done than building an entire software application from the ground up.

My hybrid system starts with a detailed scope document or statement of work. When dealing with digital projects, it is critical that you get as much detail documented up front, and that the client signs off on this document before any work begins. This document will hold everyone accountable to timelines, expectation levels, and budgets. We all know that our clients don't always get things to us in a timely fashion.

This document will give you a record that allows you to hold them accountable. If they are late in delivering items they committed to, then you document it in writing (inside the project management portal) that the project delay is a result of their late work, and due to that, the entire project timeline will be pushed back.

Detailed Scope Document

Legal Policies

It is also a very good idea to have a legal policy in place that if a client "goes dark," or is basically unresponsive, for more than 2 weeks, the entire project is to be put on hold and will be placed in a service queue to be started at the discretion of your agency. You cannot have huge delays in projects; it will crush your ability to deliver in a professional and timely fashion and will do nothing but look bad on you regardless of whose fault it truly is. This is as simple as adding a few sentences to your SLA (Service Level Agreement).

Communications

Centralized project management portal – all communications are required to go through a centralized project management portal such as teamwork, basecamp or asana. There can never be any exceptions to this rule. If a client refuses to use the portal, then you simply need to let them go elsewhere. As an agency, it is your #1 responsibility to provide professional service with measured deliverables in a timely fashion. You cannot do this unless you control the communications.

Transparent communications – it is better to have a little pain now rather than a lot of pain down the road. If for any reason you see that you cannot deliver what you promised or if the client is attempting to push the scope, you must address it in writing ASAP.

Single point in, single point out – the point of contact for both sides of the relationship (your agency and the client) need to be the only people who can harvest, decipher and transmit communications. You can't have multiple people communicating from both sides or there will be a huge web of confusion about who said what and who's responsible for what.

Meeting types – all meetings are held through a screen sharing and video conferencing tool. Gotomeeting, zoom, etc. All of these meetings are recorded and posted to the project timeline in the project management portal. When the client knows that everything is being recorded, it keeps them honest, helps to put them at ease as the project progresses forward, and if it comes down to it, saves your hide later if clients make false claims against you. MEETING

Rhythm – Weekly meetings need to be scheduled during the project calibration meeting. Every week you meet at a predefined time to discuss that week's task, milestones and objectives. These meetings are when you will make sure the client is being held accountable and your team delivers value every single week. It is important that the client sees progress every single week.

Instant Messaging – It is a good idea to have an open line of communication in an Instant Messenger application. I warn you to make sure that all communications discussed via

Instant Messenger are not official until they are logged in to the project manager platform.

Texting – Any form of open communications between you and your client is a good idea, just make sure that all of them are documented in the centralized project management platform. Also make sure that your project managers are trained to ask for clarification. In other words, if a client mentions something in a text or instant messaging, sometimes they mean to get it done and sometimes they are just brainstorming. Make sure you train them to ask if this is something they wanted added to the project scope, and that it could incur project overages, and a that change order form might have to be completed by the client.

Time Zone Allocation – Make sure you establish the time zones! Although this sounds so simple and obvious, it is amazing how often meetings get derailed as a result of missed meetings because the time zones were not discussed in the project calibration meeting.

MAP MARKER

Festering will kill your agency. Never let anything fester, good or bad. The more open, honest and proactive you are with your communications the more successful you will be. Your clients would rather hear in candid language from you rather than having to figure it out on their own over time.

How and when communications happen will determine the success or failure in life; the same holds true when managing digital projects.

Project Management Tools

Keep in mind that the tools you select will be dependent on your agency's services, project management style, and communication standards.

Every agency is unique and different; therefore, the tools you pick will also be unique and different.

We have divided the tools into three primary categories: Project Management Platforms, Online Meeting Tools, and Collaboration Tools.

Some of these tools may overlap, and many of them are designed to work together, but with some research and a little trial-and-error you should be able to find the winning combination.

Regardless of which tools you pick just remember that the ultimate goal is to improve organization, communication, and collaboration.
Having this in place will help the project lifecycle run smoothly, improve employee morale, and increase productivity.

Project Management Platforms	**Online Meeting Platforms**	**Collaboration Tools**

As always if you would like to discuss the specifics about what type of platform would best fit your agency, do not hesitate to send us an email.

Project Management Platforms

Project management platforms are intended to help the project lifecycle run as smoothly as possible. To do this, you need a platform that tracks deadlines, shares documents, and facilitates communication.

That's a pretty tall order; so picking the right platform for your agency isn't an easy task. In order to figure out what the best fit for your agency is, you will need to look at what features are good to have and what features are essential to have. Think about what features you need to deliver a project on time and within budget, as easily as possible.

Most platforms come with task management that allows you to break down big projects into milestones, tasks, and subtasks that can be assigned to specific team members, but you may need more than that.

You may need a platform that allows client access, Gantt charts, invoicing, reporting, or time logs.

Keep in mind that if they are missing just one or two key features there may be an integration that can bridge the gap.

Go through the free trial before making a final decision.

Once you train employees and clients on how to use a platform, it won't be easy to switch. So, you want to make sure you pick a platform that meets your needs, and has the ability to grow with your agency (because it's about to take off!). Below are three good picks that I have either used or owner agency owners I know have liked.

TEAMWORK: This one is my personal favorite. We used this one with my first agency and I am using it with my agency coaching business. Very user friendly, cheap, and does everything you need as it pertains to project management processes I lay out in this workbook.

BASECAMP: I used this system for years with my agency, and it worked very well. We eventually outgrow this platform because of the time tracking and reporting requirements that grow as your agency grows.

ASANA: I've never used this one, but every agency I know who has used it absolutely loves it. They like the "Boards" feature and the ease of use.

 If you are interested more information and some side by side comparisons each platform check out the resource area.

Online Meeting Platforms

Gone are the days when you had to travel to a client to meet with them. Online meeting tools allow you to talk to just about anyone from the comfort of your desk. This will help you communicate more efficiently, and depending on the platform you choose, more effectively.

When deciding on which online meeting tool to use, it's important to consider what it's going to be used for.

Will you primarily be talking to clients?
Collaborating with a remote team?
Hosting webinars?

The answers to these questions will determine how many and what kind of features you'll need.

If you're primarily dealing with clients you'll want to pick a platform that doesn't need to be downloaded and works on most browsers, you may also want a toll-free number for them to call in on.

If you're using the online meeting tool internally, then document sharing, a whiteboard, and screen sharing may be the star features. If you're hosting webinars, you may need extensive admin features that allow you to mute participants, turn off webcams, lock out latecomers, create waiting rooms, or facilitate breakout sessions.

Whatever your needs, there is an online meeting tool that will help you. The trick is finding one that also meets your budget. **Skype** is Old Faithful. It has been around forever and works well. It allows for direct phone calls and virtual phone calls, both of which are nice.

GoToMeeting is another old school solution that still works great. Not a fan of their high prices, especially when you can get everything they offer and more for a third of the cost with Zoom.

Zoom is one of my personal favorites. We use this in my agency coaching business, recording meetings, allows for everything you will need to effectively manage digital projects.

Collaboration Tools

Collaboration tools come in all shapes and sizes. Some focus on doing one thing really well, and some try to be a jack-of-all-trades. There are tools specifically created for designers, programmers, copywriters, and the list goes on. Your ideal collaboration tool will be heavily dependent on what your agency's niche and service offerings are, and it's important to remember that you may need more than one tool to get the job done. For example my staff uses G Suite to create agendas, NovaMind to plan out email campaigns, and Skype to chat!

Tool Review

The tools reviewed below suit different needs, but if you feel like they're missing something that your agency really needs then hop online, there's a tool (or Zap!) out there that will help you increase collaboration, productivity, and organization.

G SUITE – Google's business platform is my personal favorite. It syncs emails, calendars, documents, spreadsheets, and more. One of its best features is the document collaboration within Google Drive. Google Docs basic version is lacking some formatting and editing features but with a few add-ons and scripts you can be feature rich in just minutes. You also have the option to share as much, or as little, as you want. You can enable viewing, editing, or commenting permissions, and restrict downloading and printing if you need to. It shows exactly when, where, and what, people are looking at and changing on a document in real time, a truly unbeatable feature. One of the drawbacks is that organization is not native and can be a bit tedious. Other than that, it's incredibly user friendly. All of this for just a few bucks for a user to start. They also have business and enterprise packages.

QUIP – Quip is a document collaboration tool. They have cloud supported living documents and spreadsheets to make brainstorming, creating, editing and reviewing simple and synced. This means everyone always has the most updated version, and there's version tracking in case you need to go back. It comes with an integrated chat feature, push notifications, unlimited storage, privacy settings, and a mobile app. It's very user friendly, but this is largely due to the fact that it lacks so many formatting features. There is no toolbar at the top, no ruler on the page, and you can't adjust image sizes. It's naturally very organized, and facilitates communication and collaboration. You'll need the enterprise solution to unlock most of the unlimited features though and this will cost you $25 per user per month.

ALTERNATIVE DOCUMENT COLLABORATION TOOLS – Samepage, IBM Connections, Red Pen.

Slack– Slack is a beefed-up communication tool. The free plan will suit many teams' needs but has limited storage and features. The Plus package allows external guests (like your clients), group calls, two-way authentication, compliance exports, usage reports, 20 GB storage per user, customer support, and more. It has almost 500 integrations and is extremely customizable. It's most noted for its search functionality, a feature that many of its competitors are lacking. However, at $15/month per user, all of these benefits add up quickly if your agency is growing. A customizable enterprise solution is in the works, but isn't available yet.

Hipchat – This is another communication tool with fewer capabilities and a significantly lower price. For just $2/month per user you get unlimited chat rooms, drag and drop file sharing, search functionality, and push notifications. There is a lack of management control options, organization, and customization, though. There are currently about 150 integrations for Hipchat, and it's one of the few communication tools to integrate with social media and Office 365.

Other Communication Tools – Twist, Ryver, Zoho Chat, Cisco Spark.

X Mind – This mind mapping software is great for brainstorming, planning, and organizing ideas. XMind makes getting started easy with premade templates like SWOT charts, decisions trees, and timelines. It also offers task management, audio recording, and a variety of exporting options. It has a dated and clunky interface, and is slow to open. There is a very limited free version, but to unlock features you must pay the annual fee of either $79 or $129.

Mindomo – Mindomo is a cloud or desktop mind mapping software. The desktop version allows you to work offline, and will sync up when connection is restored. You can also backup your files to Google Drive or Dropbox. You can password protect maps, and even share them with guests who don't have an account. They have a 6-month licensing structure starting at $39 for one user. If your agency is growing though they have a special package for teams that enables group sharing and administrative controls.

Other Mind Mapping Tools – NovaMind, MindMeister, MindJet.

!!! Let me start by saying I am NOT an attorney!!!

All legal agreements should be vetted by your agency's attorney.

Digital Business Architect is not responsible for any legal action taken against your agency.

We are also clearly stating that the legal agreements templates we provide will not protect your agency against all potential legal liabilities.

Now that we have that out of the way, I know when I first started my agency the idea of having an attorney was a joke. I could barely afford to eat, much less have an attorney write custom legal agreements for me.

With that being said, I decided to create my own legal agreements. They worked perfectly fine while we were in the awkward growth phase of agency development. I don't want you to have to cross your fingers and hope you find good legal agreements on the web, so we have some templates that have been fine-tuned over the years that should get your agency covered for most legal liabilities.

Also keep in mind that no legal agreement can protect you from delivering sub-par services, or worse, being unethical or illegal with your agency's services and programs or communications.

So ALWAYS stay above the line and deliver world-class services and programs. If you do that, you should have very little legal issues. In case you have one of those clients (you know the one – we all have one from time to time) I've listed and defined some of the legal documents you should have prepared to keep yourself in the clear.

*The links to the templates of these agreements are in the tools and resources section of this book. Make sure to download those, customize those and then put them on your website.

Legality

For most of you, there are 5 legal documents you need to have ready to go.

1. SERVICE LEVEL AGREEMENT (SLAS) – Cover the specifics of the services you offer. If you offer a wide range of services (which I don't suggest) it is very possible you will need a few SLAs. A few things you should consider: who owns the source code, Adwords account, Facebook Ad Manager Account, Ad copy, Ad creatives, Photoshop files, who is responsible for monthly ad spending, e-commerce sites, automation platforms, and so on.

2. TERMS AND CONDITIONS – Your agency's terms and conditions outline how your fee structures work, change clause, e-commerce sites, warranties, limitation of liability, governing laws/courts, communication policies, severability clauses, payment terms, policies, procedures, client responsibilities, etc.

3. HOSTING AGREEMENT – If you offer hosting or manage your clients hosting platforms, make sure you have an agreement in place that governs and clearly outlines your agency's responsibilities and legal ownership of that account. If hosting is not a major aspect of your agency, you can easily put a few lines in your SLA to cover this potential liability.

4. PRIVACY POLICY – Outlining your agency's approach to email lists, client information, project files, meeting recordings, credit card information, cookies, etc.

5. REFUND POLICY – Outlining your agency's refund policy in clear and concise terms. A few of the items you should put in your refund policy will be administrative fees, shipping cost (if applicable), payment processing fees, etc. This agreement should be straightforward, short, and to the point.

Project Management Best Practices

1. NEVER JUMP AHEAD

2. QUALITY ASSURANCE

3. DOCUMENTED SIGN OFFS

4. NO FLUFF

5. QUICK WINS

6. OVER DOCUMENT

7. CLIENT ACCOUNTABILITY

8. TRANSPARENT COMMUNICATIONS

1. NEVER JUMP AHEAD – Regardless of how much the client begs or complains, DON'T jump ahead. If the client

MUST have something done that requires you to interrupt your service department, require that they complete a change order to make sure they understand it is a special request that falls outside of the normal scope of the project. Even if the request is something you would do in the natural flow of the project, if it goes out of turn, it will throw the timing and rhythm off for the entire project, interrupt your service department's normal rhythm, and begin the expectation that if they scream loud enough they can control your service department. It's important that they know you are the one in control.

2. QUALITY ASSURANCE – Throughout the project, you should have internal processes that are double-checking everyone's work for quality assurance issues before presenting any work to the client. This is normally done by our project managers. If you send over work that has obvious mistakes, it automatically makes your client think that you and your staff don't know what you're doing. Clearly, this could become a major issue as the project progresses forward.

3. DOCUMENTED SIGN OFFS – At the end of every phase, your agency should provide a checklist to the client. This checklist will have items on it that do not pertain to their specific project, but the goal is to get your client to think about all aspects of that phase and sign off on all aspects that pertain to their project. If there is an item on the checklist that does not pertain to their project, simply ask them to put N/A in that box.

4. NO FLUFF – The time for fluff is most definitely NOT during the project phase. During the project implementation phase, you need to make sure that your project managers are delivering the good and the bad news in candid terms.

Fluffing it up and candy-coating things will not help anybody long-term.

5. QUICK WINS – Whenever you can, deliver easy products or services that give your clients the "Quick Wins.' Even though the hard part is normally behind the scenes, there are tons of things you can do to build value as you go through the project. Do not make the mistake of working on all of the "hard" items and saving the visual or pretty items for the very end. If you do, you will allow the client to fester, which is never a good thing.

6. OVER DOCUMENT – I mentioned this in the communication phase of this workbook. We provided checklists for your clients to sign off on every phase of the project. We recommend you have a centralized project management portal that all communications are required to go through. So, just in case you have not figured out the common theme: document, document and then document again. You can never document too much, well maybe you can but it is difficult.

7. CLIENT ACCOUNTABILITY – Never forget that your agency is only as good as the information/feedback it receives. If a client says, "Just get it done," you need to politely remind them that they hired a professional group, and as with all successful relationships it takes two to be wildly successful. Make sure they are giving you feedback, providing you with the required materials and login credentials required to successfully fulfill their business dreams.

8. TRANSPARENT COMMUNICATIONS – I know I'm beating this to death, but I hope that shows you how important it is. Transparency will instill within your clients an unsaid confidence in your organization. They can feel that your agency is being "above the line" every step of the way. This alone got me out of hot water so many times. When your agency makes a mistake (which tends to happen more and more as your agency grows) and you have been 100% transparent throughout the entire project and you haven't "fluffed" things up to make your agency look better in the short-term, the client will forgive almost anything.

8 STEP PROJECT MANAGEMENT PERFECT LIFECYCLE

In this chapter's section, we cover the 8 steps required to effectively manage a digital project.

Your agency's structure will determine how each of these phases manifests themselves for your specific service offerings. Regardless of what your service offerings are, the project management life cycle should look very similar to the 8 steps outlined in this section.

Each section is intended to build value, receive documented approval at specific milestones, and protect your agency from large project liabilities (refunds, chargebacks, legal disputes, etc.).

* To help you get this 8-step process in place as fast as possible, we created checklists specifically for your clients for each phase as well as an internal progress checklist timeline spreadsheet to ensure all aspects of your projects go smoothly, and no steps are skipped by accident (See resources for details)

1. PROJECT CALIBRATION – This meeting will set the tone for the entire project and should be taken very seriously. In the resources/tools section of the course we provide a checklist for this phase. Download that tool, customize it for your agency and get it implemented ASAP. If you are working on a custom project, you will need to create a detailed project scope document before any work begins. In the resources/tools section we provide a template scope document.

2. COPYWRITING – Whether the client provides the copy, or you were hired to write the copy, you need to make sure you outline the exact pages required to effectively create a website, or the exact amount of ad copy, email copy, and so on. I would also suggest creating a spreadsheet that list all of the items your agency is responsible for and columns for each phase of completion.

3. DESIGN – Designing concepts for a website, ad, or landing page all follow the same approval process. I like to call it the Version 1 (V1), Version 2 (V2), and Rock On process (just for fun!). During the design phase, you need to make sure the client understands they get two edit rounds for all design creative concepts and after that they may incur additional charges. Before this process was implemented in my agency, we would have clients ask to see 50 different shades of purple, just so they could make it "perfect" in their eyes.

After we implemented this process, instead of getting off the wall design edit requests, we started receiving detailed lists of exactly what they wanted to see, they would meet with their staff to make sure everyone had their input before sending us those edits, and as a result, we'd make much faster decisions as it pertains to the design process. The size of the project will determine the scale of process you need in the design phase. If it's a massive project, you might need to implement a wireframe phase.

This means, you submit a framework made up of boxes that have no color and require the client to make decisions about where they want the actual content of their design before they fall in love with their brand palette. Now, if it is a website from a template, then you could simply implement the copy into the WordPress theme and submit a working concept. Regardless of how you do it, make sure you limit the amount of edits they have and hold them accountable as it pertains to providing thought through checklists for edits. Let them dream, but if all they want to do is dream, they need to pay extra for that. DigitalBusinessArchitects.com

4. DEVELOPMENT/CAMPAIGN CREATION – In the digital world, this can literally mean just about anything. Whether it is custom programming a website, landing page or automation campaign, or it is implementing a WordPress theme with some basic CSS styling. The process is pretty similar, never submit programming work to the client without having at least 2 internal quality assurance steps, provide a checklist for the client to follow and ALWAYS keep a very close eye on scope creep. This is typically when they start to dream about building Facebook for the underwater basket weaving community.

5. BETA TESTING AND BETA CHECKLIST – We provided a checklist for all phases, including this one. Make sure you download it and follow that format when creating a beta checklist for your projects. Also, if you are doing your job, the beta checklist should be short and address 99.9% of all concerns, therefore making the final testing and checklist phase more of a formality than anything else.

6. FINAL TESTING AND FINAL CHECKLIST – As I mentioned, this phase should be a formality and a stopgap measure to make sure nothing fell through the cracks. Make sure everything is perfect and exactly as your client wants it.

7. CLIENT TRAINING – If you are in media buying (Facebook Ads, Google Ads, etc.) this phase will most likely not pertain to you. Unless you want to train them on how to view your reports, or something of the like. If you are in the website or automation business, this will most likely apply to you. Think about all of the items your client needs to know to be successful. Make sure you use this phase to build value in ongoing services and that this phase leaves the client with a huge smile on their face.

8. GO LIVE – Again, depending on your agency's core service offerings, the exact details you put into your "Go Live" checklist could vary, but don't overlook this phase. Before you go live, do one more final test, double check DNS and MX records, Ad Spends, Keyword Inserts and then have the client sign off on the fact that everything is okay and ready to go! As with the other phases, we have a checklist for you to review, take that template and customize it to your agency's needs.

Upon the completion of all phases there must be a sign off process and most phases should be accompanied with instructions or a checklist for the client to guide them through the process of checking your work. In the resources and tools section we provided an example Sign-Off sheet for the Copy Phase, which looks like the image below.

When managing a service department and project managers there are a few best manage practices I'd like to share with you.

1. FLY BY NUMBERS – Use the KPI spreadsheets we provide in our Agency Performance Indicators lesson to keep a pulse on all the things that pertain to your service department and make adjustments to your systems that are based on hard data rather than guesswork.

2. TRUST BUT VERIFY – Always have an automated follow up process that checks in on your service department's performance. Send customer satisfaction surveys periodically during the process, do random phone calls to clients, and ask them how everything is going.

3. INBOX ZERO POLICY – It is a good idea to train your project managers to have a zero inbox policy. Before they can leave for the day, they must have addressed all emails, phone calls and messages. Never leave anything open ended, always address it immediately.

4. ACTIVE PROJECT INVENTORY CHECK – It is a good idea to have a 30-minute end of the day project status update. In this meeting you allow each PM to go over the happenings of the day and bring up any items of concern (labor allocations, resources, bugs, etc.). You should also have a weekly meeting where you go through every single projects in detail, this meeting will last 1-3 hours depending on how many active projects you have. You should have an agenda for this meeting, and every PM should know that they will be required to have a detailed status report for every single project.

5. PROBLEM CHILDREN AUDIT PROCESS – As much as we would like to think we will never have any problems, we all know that is not how it actually turns out. There will always be problem children and projects. Make sure you have the ability to audit your team's performance in detail and make sure they understand that you are the professional services group; one mistake by your staff is more than enough for your client to scream "Foul!" and hold you over a barrel for free work.

You reflect on your team's performance and make minor changes to constantly improve and learn from those mistakes.

8. ATTA BOYS & ATTA GIRLS – Being the front line defender (PM) for your brand is a tough and often thankless position to be in. Make sure you, as their boss, are their biggest cheerleader and ALWAYS have their back. If they make a mistake, you own that mistake publicly and then privately you can use it as a learning tool. NEVER throw your staff under the bus publicly!

9. PERFORMANCE REWARDS – Say thank you to your service department leaders often and give them small gifts showing your appreciation for the dedication and hard work. Let them know how valuable they are to your agency, because make no mistake about it, without badass PMs, you would still be doing all the service on your own.

10. IN THE TRENCHES – Never be afraid to dive into the trenches with your staff, but make sure you don't come in and take control of it. You should simply offer a lending hand just like another employee, ask if you can get them coffee, take out their trash or work late to help them get caught up on emails.

11. PATH TO PROSPERITY – All employees like to know they have a path to grow, make sure this path is clearly outlined in an organizational chart or something similar. Show them the future and bring them into the planning for the future; the payoff is huge!

12. CELEBRATE SUCCESS – When you deliver on a huge project that everyone rallied around, take the team out for dinner or a white-water rafting trip. Find something fun and NON-work related to celebrate your team's success.

Project Management Wrap Up

WRAP UP

This section is probably the hardest one we had to create...

The number of variables involved in project management are endless, the number of products/services agencies offer are endless, and we want to guarantee you an ironclad project management process that eliminates scope creep, protects you legally, and allows you to handle explosive growth going forward.

Countless hours of experience, research and teamwork went into providing you the absolute best project management framework for digital agencies in the world.

Not only did we want to provide the project management framework, but we also wanted to provide the actual tools and legal documents required.

If you follow the best management practices, hybrid methodology outlined, and the 8- step process, you will catapult past your competitors in the blink of an eye.

As with all of the tools and toolboxes in the Agency Blueprint, they are intended to be used in tandem with each other. Download all of the templates provided, they will be everything you need to get your project management processes iron clad in the next 3-4 weeks.

Implementing this process will be difficult at first, but don't give up. Stick to it and constantly make modifications in weekly meetings. The kick-start you get from this chapter will push you years forward from your current position. Once you modify the advice specifically to your agency's needs over the course of a few months, you will have a world-class service infrastructure custom to spark your agency's explosive growth.

MONTH NINE

In month nine, you're going to learn how to turn your agency into an automated or 'systematized' business... While maintaining a high standard of quality.

.

Chapter 9

Sales and Marketing Automation

Once your business has put in place all of the techniques of previous chapters and your business is going to grow. you will hit a plateau unless you can transition away from doing custom personalized work and toward an automated or systematized business.

Learn how to scale your agency by driving leads, harvesting those leads and then converting them into happy paying clients – all done with automation independently of the agency owner in a systematized format with predictable results.

As with all successful businesses, sales and marketing is the lifeblood and will determine the level of success, failure, and buyout evaluations. To scale your agency, it will require the ability to drive leads, harvest those leads and then convert them into happy paying clients. All of this has to be done independently of the agency owner and it has to be systematized with predictable results. Everything in this workbook is intended to outline a proven sales automation and management system that worked miracles for my first agency.

The processes and systems outlined in this workbook are intended to accomplish the following:

Ensure that all leads are **harvested and nurtured**, Provide **precise agency performance indicators**, Provide a **proven** sales pipeline management system, **Increase lead-to-close percentages**, **Lower media buying budgets** over time, **Lower labor** required in running and managing a sales department, **Standardize a sales and marketing system** for your agency, **Increase brand penetration** in your target audience, & **Imprint your brand** into your prospects' long term memory – Become a trusted source

90% of all your interactions with prospects and clients, as it pertains specifically to sales and marketing, should be automated or in an automated CRM platform. From the time a prospect raises his or her hand to the time you are asking for referrals, the entire process should be thought out, mapped out in detail, and closely tracked in a Customer Relationship Management application like Infusionsoft, HubSpot or any other advanced CRM platform that has advanced automation features.

In this chapter, I am going to outline the systems that you need to get in place for your agency in order to make effectiveness and efficiency with automation a reality for your organization.

The guiding philosophy behind harvesting your target audience's data, eliminating follow up failure, and a sales pipeline management process is "Brand Penetration." I learned this formula from one of my marketing mentors, Jay Conrad Levinson (Father of Guerrilla Marketing). While teaching digital marketing at one of his intensive training courses, he taught me this simple brand penetration formula that still works wonders to this day

Based upon the amount of times a prospect has interacted with your agency, this is how that prospect would respond if a friend were to ask their opinion on your agency

You'll notice that nothing has changed in each of these scenarios except the fact that they have seen your brand (had your brand imprinted) into their memory with more frequency.

There is a survival mechanism deep inside of our brains that transfers information from our short term to our long-term memory after it has been seen a certain number of times (the number of times is debatable, depends on the level of emotion involved). As you can see, the name of the game is to get your brand in front of your target audience as often as possible.

The golden rule is to make sure you get your brand in front of your prospects as many times as possible. The more emotion you can associate to your brand the more likely they will remember it. Whether through high emotion or through high value content repeated over time, your interactions can have a lasting effect on your prospects.

Once a prospect has been introduced to your brand in a high value way **at least 7–9 times**, the triggering mechanism in the brain shifts your brand from short-term (which gets wiped clean every night) into long-term (where we store the more trusted sources of information for bigger decisions).

1-3
POSITIVE INTERACTIONS WITH YOUR BRAND

"I have heard of that agency, but I don't know much about them."

4-6
POSITIVE INTERACTIONS WITH YOUR BRAND

"I have heard of that agency, and I hear they do good work, but I've never used them."

7-9
POSITIVE INTERACTIONS WITH YOUR BRAND

"I have heard of that agency, and I hear they do good work. If I ever need an agency, that's who I'll call first."

Once this happens, you are now imprinted onto your prospects' mind. When they are in the market for digital/social media marketing, they will recall your name, seek out an email address or phone number, or they'll Google search your agency's name.

Why do you think all of the huge companies (national brands) spend so much money on Super Bowl ads? The emotion behind the game is high, so they know their commercial will shift their agency to our long-term memory. We always discuss those commercials for weeks after the game – sometimes even longer than we discuss the game itself. Therefore, when their prospects need their services they will recall their brand and reach out.

You, as a smaller agency, can now have the same impact.

You must harvest all data, implement a sales pipeline, and follow up with them through the use of automation, or else it'll be more work than you're physically able to perform.

The Object Oriented Planning System O.O.P.S

As you develop the 6 topics we cover in this book, it is important that you have everything clean, organized, and easy to find down the road.

Lead Harvesting	New Client Nurturing
Sales Pipeline Automation Management	Client Satisfaction
Prospect Nurturing	Evergreen and Holiday Nurturing

We created a simple system that we highly recommend to other agency owners.

It is a numbers-based naming convention that categorizes everything into unique objects and daisy chains them together into a comprehensive client path.

This system is the Object Oriented Planning System (OOPS).

You'll see that I use it when naming campaigns and tags throughout this document.

The idea behind this system is that you create a lot of campaigns similarly organized to the tags in your customer relationship management system.

I know at first this sounds crazy, but when you have the ability to give a niche/genre/category a specific numerical range and naming convention it really enables you to find things and logically connect the pieces of your sales funnel in a numerical way.

You can now easily search for items, train employees, and create standardized processes on how and why things are managed, as well as who is managing them based on certain employees taking ownership of specific numerical categories. If only one person knows how to use your CRM, what would happen if there was an emergency and that person is unable to be reached?

In the resources section of this book you will find a where to access a workbook that explains this in much more detail. We also created an entire lesson around this system.

The 6 topics I am about to teach you in this book are all intended to empower your agency for explosive long term and sustainable growth:

Lead Harvesting Sales Pipeline Automation Management Prospect

Nurturing New Client Nurturing Client Satisfaction Evergreen and Holiday Nurturing

In our membership we provide you with detailed mind maps, examples, email copy and lecture training videos on exactly how to get all 6 of these sales and marketing automated systems in place for your agency. Take the huge step and do the hard work, these systems will revolutionize how you run your agency's sales machine!

1000 - Lead Harvesting (Mini Intro) Campaigns – As an agency you need at least 4–5 lead magnets that harvest leads from your website, social media, publications or live events. All of these magnets should have automated nurturing campaigns associated to them. Here are a few of the more common lead magnets (call to actions or CTAs), but get creative and make sure you customize these to your specific niche and geographical area.

Client Results Pages – Prospects care about one thing: results. Give them what they want. Have client results pages, case studies, a chat module on those pages to ask questions, etc.

Free 1 Hour Consult – This one always converted more sales than anything else, it might sound cheesy, but it produces highly profitable sales.

Contact Us Page – I know you have one of these already. However, on your Contact Us page, people who opt in through this form are usually more engaged and are ready to get a proposal.

Ask them the right questions out of the gate and get to know them better from the start.

Free Top 10 Tips – Businesses still love getting free tips, so for the prospects who are just "checking" out agencies now for a project down the road will opt into something like this. Give them top 10 social media tips, marketing automation tips, etc.

Phone Number – I know this sounds like a DUH, but it amazes me how often

The Lead Harvesting Campaign is intended to deliver the lead magnet, harvest all agency performance data and kick off the sales pipeline management process. To visually illustrate how this process should flow, I created a mind map that outlines the specifics; here is a screenshot of that mind map. The link to how to access this mind map in high-resolution version is available in the resources section.

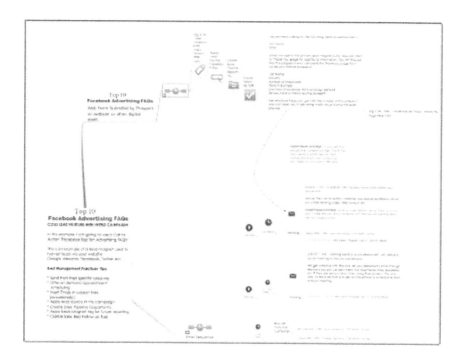

As you can see this is a very simple campaign that ensures all the data is harvested, you deliver exactly what you promised (and more if you're smart) and attempt to get a meeting scheduled ASAP.

This campaign lasts 48–72 hours typically, then it hands it off to the "2000 – Prospect Nurturing Campaign" to continue the education and trust building phase of the sales cycle.

Your agency should have a unique *"1000 – Lead Harvesting (Mini Intro) Campaign"* for every call to action on your website, every event you attend, every webinar you host or speak on and for each media buying channel where you purchase traffic.

It might sound like a lot of work and effort, but the reality is that once you get the first one set up, all you have to do is clone the original 1000 level campaign once it's completely finished and customize the information for that specific call to action, event, or whichever channel.

The goal is to build a database of your target audience in your local area or niche. It is critical that you harvest as much data as possible; the agency with the ability to contact their target audience for the cheapest possible cost will win in the end.

You can take this data, upload it to social media platforms and target them via Social Media, email, direct mail and run an outbound phone call campaign.

Once they raise their hand and express an interest in hiring your agency, all leads become a hot prospect. All prospects need to be entered into your sales pipeline and prospect nurturing campaign –we will get into the prospect nurturing campaigns shortly. This is one of the biggest mistakes I see in the growth of an agency or businesses in general. A lot of agency owners are in charge of the sales and they do not see it as a priority, but that is a HUGE mistake.

There are dozens of reasons, but the top few are; accountability, automated follow up and the data it provides over time is priceless when planning to grow your sales departments

MAP MARKER

If you ever intend on selling your agency, having a sales process/pipeline tracking system is very valuable to a potential buyer. It can increase the evaluation of your agency by 2X or 3X.

Sales Pipeline

If you haven't used one before, think of a sales pipeline as a visual representation of your prospects as they are led through the purchasing process.

We use the term "client path" to describe where your prospects go from the second they first interact with your agency at the lead source all the way to leaving reviews and sending over referrals.

There are a lot of ways to manage a sales pipeline, but the most efficient way is to use a cloud-based customer relationship management application.

These applications allow you to centralize your data, scale your sales staff, and harvest precise agency performance indicators that allow you to improve or scale your sales efforts easily.

Some CRM platforms have wonderful sales pipeline management systems, but they do not contain pipeline automation.

I HIGHLY suggest you get a CRM platform that has automation integrated natively, like HubSpot or Infusionsoft

Both have free or a very cheap version that provide the sales pipeline features in them.

You should customize Some CRM platforms have wonderful sales pipeline management systems, but they do not contain pipeline automation. I HIGHLY suggest you get a CRM platform that has automation integrated natively, like

HubSpot or Infusionsoft. Both have free or a very cheap version that provide the sales pipeline features in them. To the right there is an example of what a sales pipeline should look like.

The example I provide is just that, an example.

You should customize the pipeline to fit your specific agencies requirements. Whether you're a social media, creative, programming or full-service agency the process is a little different for each.

The pipeline to fit your specific agencies requirements. Whether you're a social media, creative, programming or full-service agency the process is a little different for each.

Sales Pipeline 7-Step Foundation

1. New Opportunity – Any new lead that enters into your agency, phone calls, website, social media.

2. Left Voicemail/Trying to get in Touch – Once a phone number has been harvested and asked to talk to a rep.

3. Phone/Establishing a Need – A phone meeting has been held and both parties align in reference to their demand and your ability to supply.

4. Meeting/Establishing the Details – This is a predefined meeting to outline the scope of the project and to get into the details of what the prospect is expecting.

5. Closing/Proposal has been Submitted – A proposal has been submitted and it is time to get an answer, always require an answer, even if it's a "No."

6. Won – As you'd expect, this is when you win a prospect and it's time to kick off the New Client Nurturing campaign and celebrate!

7. Lost – When a prospect goes with another vendor or you lost the deal for any reason. All seven of these steps can (and should) have numerous different steps within each phase, but regardless of how many steps you setup, it should follow this basic 7-step foundation.

Pipeline Automation

By saving time and standardizing the sales follow up process, you as the owner can expect measured results and higher productivity out of your sales department.

Pipeline automation accomplishes three BIG things.

1. Requires you, the owner, to standardize your phone and email follow up processes.

2. Requires your sales reps to follow a strict sales process.

3. Saves your sales reps a TON of time.

This allows you to predict the amount of sales coming into your service department and then turn up the heat based upon bandwidth available.

After running sales through a sales pipeline automation process for 4–6 months you will see exactly how many leads you are really getting, how many referrals you're getting, and what your sales reps closing percentages are.

All of these agency performance indicators are critical in scaling your agency past the 7/8-figure mark.

The two primary components you need to focus on are the email automated follow up and the task/calendar management automation features.

Both of these features are engaged when the sales rep moves a prospect from one sales stage to another sales stage, therefore triggering the automated sales pipeline system to take action.

Sales Stage Triggers

These are very simple and can be setup in a matter of minutes, here is an example of what the triggers look like in my CRM application. Notice I set up the triggers and then configure them to do the specific automation items I need done in that specific phase of the sales process.

Pipeline Automation Emails

Emails sent out when a sales rep moves a prospect from one sales stage to another sales stage in a sales pipeline management system. These emails should be simple and give the prospect numerous options to get back in touch with the sales rep. Prospects are busy and will take the option that best fits the situation they are in at that time, so give them as many options as possible to communicate with your sales reps.

Here are some examples.

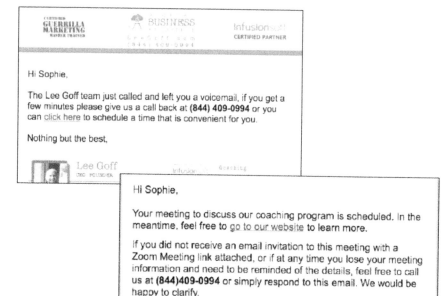

As you can see it is a very simple reminder that you called and you are working hard to earn their business.

Follow up is all about educating, trust building and showing them that you will work hard for their business. In conjunction with tracking everything in a visual sales pipeline dashboard, you also send automated emails. The next step is to set up automated tasks to remind you to call them again in a few days.

All of this saves you a ton of time. If your agency is to the point of having numerous sales reps, you can now track if those sales reps are completing their tasks on time, how many emails are sent out, and if they are moving prospects along the pipeline in a timely manner. **Here is a simple example of how you can set up an automated task reminder**.

Again, keep it simple, do not overthink it, and just get it in place and tweak it over time. In most instances, "done" is better than "perfect.

You should configure what type of follow up is in order:

1. Explain the task details in the body,
2. Assign it to the rep and a back up rep,
3. Set a due date,
4. Decide on prospect priority,
5. Notify the contact owner, and
6. Set up desired outcomes and automated sequences to kick off based upon predefined outcomes.

When you aggregate all of those repetitive tasks over 20–50 calls a week, it is a massive time saver. Also, it guarantees that your brand is in front of the prospect at least twice for every single phone call with the automated emails, holds your sales reps accountable, gives you precise sales agency performance indicators, and can automate a portion of the new customer on-boarding process. One of the residual benefits is that it also forces you to standardize the entire process, which will make your sales staff more efficient, and make your agency's buyout evaluation increase substantially.

MAP MARKER

I have said it before, but it is so important I am saying it again: start simple. Do not overthink this process, do not attempt to account for every type of sales scenario, keep the sales pipeline stages extremely simple, and get the sales staff to buy in to the process before tweaking it and making it more detailed. Start small, get staff buy in, and then let the staff help you build out a fine tuned Ferrari!

2000 - Prospect Nurturing Campaign – A campaign that educates prospects on who your agency is, presents them with social proof, social trust, community ties, and introduces them to the CEO. Each of these items is instrumental in the education and trust building phases of the sales process. As the agency owner, you do not want individual sales reps creating answers to these questions. You must control the conversation with video, email and automated follow up. If you produce the content that the prospect receives, it will set the tone for all conversations held by your sales staff. If they start to adlib a little too much, the prospect will bring up the video and/or email. You will find this to be an extremely effective accountability and training tool for your sales departments.

On average, it lasts about 30–60 days depending on the average buy cycle for your agency.

Upon the completion of this campaign, if the prospect did not purchase they will be transitioned into the 3000 - Evergreen/Holiday Campaign for long term nurturing. If the prospect does purchase from you, you should have a campaign set up that stops the prospect nurturing campaign and engages the "New Client Nurturing" campaign.

Once that campaign has run its course, that's when you engage the evergreen/holiday campaign for long term nurturing. I highly recommend you use that as a road map to create your agency's own customized prospect nurturing campaign.

Low-Res Prospect Nurturing Campaign Mind Map Illustration Example

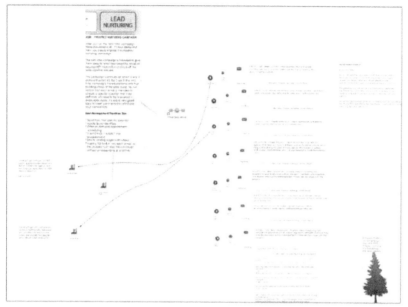

New Client Nurturing – A campaign that outlines all aspects of the project. The new client nurturing campaign should contain the following items:

Introduction to Their Team Members – It is difficult to introduce the exact team members to the client via an automated email or video, but you can introduce them to key team members that will be a part of their project. Produce a video and let the individual departments speak for a couple of minutes explaining who they are and what they do for the client.

Project Kick Off Process – Explain that we have a predefined project kick off process that sets everyone up for success. This kick off meeting is when you will meet the specific members of your team

Communication Standards – Typically explained during the project kick off meeting. You make sure the client understands that you only receive direction from one person on their team (cannot get into the situation of receiving direction from numerous people) and that all communications must go through the project management portal or it will not get put into the service queue.

Escalation Process – Let them know that if they are ever not happy with any aspect of their project that they always have the option to call the CEO directly to express any concerns or possible improvements to the project management process.

Project Management Portal Training – Produce a quick training video for the client to watch or share with key team members on their side of the project. Normally there is a quick training during the project kick off meeting, but it is always a good idea to give them a video for refresher, etc.

Change Order Process – Explain to them that you have a precise timeline and budget that your agency takes very serious, because you are passionate about delivering their dreams on time and on budget. Now if they have special request during the project that have never been discussed or introduced in writing, then there will be change orders produced for the client to sign off on before any additional work can be scheduled, billed or allocated for in the timeline.

Refund Policies – Explain to them in detail what your refund policy is. I would strongly advise you that you outline this is great detail, clients can really get pushy if it gets to the refund my money level.

This is almost always a point of contention and the more outlined it is, the safer your agency will be protected against unreasonable refund request.

Sales and Service Calibration – This is normally done during the project kick off meeting, but regardless of when it happens, the project cannot go forward until it happens. This is when a sale, service, and the client all come together to discuss the scope of the project. Everyone must agree in writing that the sales and service set identical expectation levels for the project, so the client doesn't have any confusion going forward.

Legal Requirements – Some agency owners leave this section out, they feel like it is introducing a negative into the project. I personally like to remind the client of the legal documents they agreed in a very polite and non-pushy manner.

New Client Nurturing/Onboarding Campaign

Client Satisfaction Survey, Reviews and Referrals Campaign – At the end of all projects, the project manager should kick off a campaign that engages the client in a positive manner asking them to complete a satisfaction survey.

There are 4 primary components you need to keep in mind while building this campaign:

1. All satisfaction surveys should be seen by leadership, who should provide feedback on those surveys.

2. If there is a 3-star or below rating, bounce them to a page explaining that anything below a 4 star review is completely unacceptable and a member of the leadership team will be contacting them within 24 hours.

3. If the client gives your agency 4 or 5 stars, then bounce them to a page where they can leave a review.

4. One of the questions in the satisfaction survey should ask them if they like your agency's services enough to recommend your agency to a friend. If they answer yes to this question and give your agency a rating of 4 or 5 after the leave a review page you should redirect them to a refer a friend page. If they do not give you a referral, I would suggest

sending another email in 30 days incentivizing them with something small (gift cards are a good option).

I also recommend using systems like SoTellUs or Podium for the automated management of the client review process. There are tons of systems out there to help make this process easy, and most importantly, help you manage the positive and negative reviews (although there should never be any negative reviews).

*In the resources and tools section of this book, there is an example of how a Client Satisfaction Survey, Reviews and Referrals Campaign should look like.

Evergreen/Holiday Campaign – Make sure you have at least 2 years of automated emails ready to roll out for all cold leads who are not ready within the first 30-90 days of opting in to your lead magnets. The evergreen/holiday campaign will also apply for all prospects who sign up to be a client, but it will begin after they have gone through the new client onboarding campaign.

The evergreen/holiday campaign is intended to supplement a monthly newsletter and a monthly promotional email. You will notice that the evergreen and holiday campaigns are actually independent campaigns that run-in coordination with each other.

I do not recommend putting too much thought on exactly when certain emails are going out. If you make your emails engaging, educational, and fun it does not matter if a couple of emails go out on adjacent days.

Best Management Practice Considerations

• **Have a mini campaign that notifies a sales rep when someone takes action** (clicks a link) in an evergreen email. This is a good indicator that they are interested in learning more about that topic and a quick phone call to that individual is a great way to get leads consistently.

• **Monitor the daily activity report for cold leads** clicking more than one email, if you are monitoring this consistently you will be able to recognize when someone is about to resurface for a proposal. Keep a close eye on the activity report and use it as a reason to keep in touch with your prospect base.

• **Do not attempt to automate everything in your evergreen/holiday campaign**, you should have on average one email from the high value campaign and one email from the holiday campaign go out each month. The rest of the month you should send out a monthly newsletter and one promotional email, but this can vary to fit your specific agencies service, client and personality types.

That wraps up the sales and marketing automation part of our book. This month I suggest you start with the intro campaigns, move on to building out the prospect nurturing campaigns, and then move down the line. I know this is a lot of work, but nothing worth having is ever easy. If you want a sustainable and profitable agency, this is one of the critical systems you must get in place.

We have provided the mind maps for everything, examples of how to configure them, example email copy, and kick ass content creation resources and ideas.

 *There are mind maps available. Find links to get access, in the resources section -they are customizable to your agency's marketing needs'

Sales and Marketing Automation Wrap Up

 Now get busy! Remember to delegate work to trusted team members.

Create a list of people you want to help you tackle this project. You'll need people writing copy and inputting emails and tasks into your CRM system.

Let's get your agency to the next level.

MONTH TEN

In this chapter you will learn how to ensure you're agency is on the right track as you move toward a wholly automated agency…

Chapter 10

Key Performance Indicators

I've laid out a plan to properly test and track your success. As well as how to be as effective and efficient as possible with your marketing dollars by looking at hard data that shows you what is working and what isn't.

Step 1: Identifying The Indicators

Performance Indicators are quantifiable measurements used to evaluate a company's success over time. These are values such as inventory turnover, COGS (cost of goods sold), revenue growth rate, cash flow forecast, relative market share, etc. Every industry and every stage of business needs to use different performance metrics to accurately gauge its success.

So, how do you determine which ones to spend time on and where **do you even start?**

I developed the agency performance indicators course to tell you everything you need to know when it comes to measuring your agency's growth and success. We've narrowed it down into three easy categories that work specifically for digital marketing agencies, this way you don't have to waste your precious time **guessing.**

You'll hear me and others say, "If it's not being tracked, it's not happening."
This means that if you don't know what to attribute your success to, you can't repeat it. Which means it essentially means nothing to you or to your agency because it won't ever be a long-term solution. KPIs are in place to teach you what works best for your agency – increasing both your efficiency and your effectiveness overall.

Following this guide and utilizing the tools and resources we provided will help you get one step closer to growing an agency that isn't tethered to you.

Agency performance indicators will allow you to know exactly how your business is doing without having to get involved in the daily operations.

These may take a couple weeks or months to get established and working well but trust the process and you will see how eye-opening the numbers can be.

Explosive growth is just a few months and a little elbow grease away, so let's get going!

As I've said before, in marketing, and in business in general, if it's not being tracked, it did not happen. One of the biggest mistakes I see in agencies is failing to track the critical items that determine success or failure.

You've probably heard the saying:

"If you don't know where you are going, you'll end up someplace else." – Yogi Berra

Or maybe you've heard this one:

"Those who fail to learn from history are doomed to repeat it." – George Santayana (but made famous by Winston Churchill)

Both of these statements essentially mean the same thing: Move with intent, track everything, analyze it, learn from it, and get better with every action you take.

Obviously, this isn't something you don't already know, but maybe you got too busy trying to put out fires right and left to be able to make it a priority.

The truth is, tracking the key data in your agency has to be a priority. You might ask, "But how do I track everything? When should I track everything? And most importantly, what do I do with the data that I am tracking?" Or you might be thinking, "I am so busy I can barely find time to see my friends and family. How am I supposed to track everything? I'm trying hard enough just to survive and keep my head above water!" Yet, that is exactly why you need to track everything. If you don't, you could be repeating a ton of mistakes, wasting time, and throwing your profits in the trash.

The first time I go through the **Agency Performance Indicator** exercises, my coaching clients respond similarly, "Do you seriously expect me to have time to manage all this extra work when I'm already barely keeping myself afloat?"

And I respond with, "**YES!**"

I also recommend that someone other than you harvest the KPI data and presents it to you in a consistent pattern (rhythm).

This is a healthy way to begin the delegation process.

All of this "extra work" up front leads to relaxation and free time later down the road. The initial investment of time and work is well worth the reward.

If you faithfully stick to tracking your profits for just 3 months, you'll see why I put so much emphasis on tracking everything you do.

If you take the time to make measuring profits as part of your agency rhythm, you can expect to gain three things:

Focus
Concentrate your efforts on what really matters.

Clarity
Know exactly where your money is coming from.

Fulcrum
Use what you've learned to become *proactive*.

Focus
Concentrate your efforts on what really matters

Clarity
Know exactly where your money is coming from

Fulcrum
Use what you've learned to become *PROACTIVE*

Well, how do you eat an elephant? One bite at a time! Just get started and stick to it for at least 90 days (more than a month, sorry)

Step 2: The First 3 Things To Track

First, let's break your finances down into three primary categories:

1. Expenses You must know where every penny is going by diligently recording everything you spend your money on. This will allow you to cut an estimated 5-10% off of your expenses. With a detailed record of your expenses, you'll be able to see what's really important and what isn't.

2. Revenue This doesn't refer to how much money came into the bank account at the end of each month. This means knowing where the money came from, how it got there, and how you can get more of it from the same or a similar well. You need to know how much came from residual income, project work, referral fees and pass through project work.

3. Customer Acquisition Cost (CAC) Try not to think of this as an expense. Instead, CAC refers to finding leads, closing those leads, and then creating paying customers. This should be at the top of the list if you're thinking of scaling or selling your agency. Your success will be determined by how much it costs you to get business in the door. This is much more detailed than simply throwing it in as a line item under the expense's category.

Step 3: Tracking Expenses

Payroll   *Office Operations*

Payroll - You need to be able to break payroll down granularly by department, by employee, and by pay period – to the point that you know how much each employee costs individually. That way, you can compare each employee's cost to the revenue they bring in once you get your entire Performance Indicators System implemented.

Office Operations - This is everything else, and I mean everything else: your Internet bill, electricity bill, your network, office supplies, loans, insurance, etc. As you could imagine, this category must also be broken down into tiny line items (because if it stood alone, it'd be a whale). Break it down into categories like utilities, administrative, legal, etc.

Some of the less obvious expense items are your internal labor cost, billable labor cost, labor efficacy numbers, billable days per month, the list goes on!

As you begin measuring profits in greater detail you will start to see areas that need more attention. Eventually you will be able to forecast service bandwidth issues, cash flow issues, just about anything that could get in the way of your goals. It is such an empowering thing to know where your money is going.

Residual

Project

Residual - How much of your cash flow is on a retainer or monthly payment basis?

You need to know exact percentages and track them closely. I have seen many great agencies fail because they lost a few big retainer clients and couldn't afford payroll.

Don't make this mistake. Know how much you can afford to lose and still stay afloat.

Project - How much of your monthly income comes from larger projects? Typically, this is the big-ticket item, the one that allows you to pay off mortgages and get your kids into private school. However, it can also be the one to sink you if you don't manage it properly or know how much manpower is required.

You need to set a healthy percentage to each category and stick to it! Some agencies run perfectly at 30% residual and 70% project based.

If your agency is strictly a traffic generation agency (media buying) it is possible to have exclusively residual based income. If this is your agency, be very careful not to have a few "Big Fish" clients. Make sure you have a healthy balance between large and small clients. Failure to do so could cause severe damage and may cause you to go out of business.

Understanding what kind of revenue, you have and how much of each type of revenue your infrastructure can handle will balance out those peaks and valleys. Stabilizing those peaks and valleys will put you in a position to scale your agency because you will know exactly what moves create the most value for your business.

Step 4: Tracking Revenue

Peaks and valleys in an agency can be very difficult to balance out, but if you track exactly where your revenue is coming from and how much profit each line of revenue produces, you can eliminate those valleys and ride high on the peak of success.

Another agency performance indicator you need to consider tracking is how much "new sales" revenue versus "existing client" revenue your infrastructure can handle at any one time.

If you have too many new clients come on board in a short period of time, it will bottleneck your service infrastructure and cause severe quality issues, delayed deliverable dates, and eventually lead to angry clients. **None of which you want.**

The more you can manage a healthy percentage of new clients versus existing clients in your service infrastructure, the more smoothly your agency will run.

These are just a few examples of why tracking your agency performance indicators is so critical. Get started today and don't stop until you gain the clarity to focus on the profit producing tasks or clients.

Step 5: Tracking Customer Acquisition Costs

Lead Harvesting

Lead Nurturing

Lead Harvesting

Most people know this as the "Lead Source." However, most business owners don't know how to track all the way back to the beginning to find exactly what they spent to get those leads.

Which videos, free reports, surveys, quizzes, etc. are converting best?

You will need to track items like these under expenses as "internal" time and associate it to the lead-harvesting category.

What types of materials are bringing in the most traffic to your site?

Which materials get the hotter leads that close the bigger deals you want?

You want to be able to recreate your success and get even higher closing percentages.

Lead Nurturing

Commonly referred to as the "sales cycle" or the "buy cycle." Every agency has an average sales cycle, and the less time it takes to close leads, the more profitable you will become. When I say, "close them faster," I don't mean skipping critical aspects of the psychology of the sale. You must inform your prospects, get them to trust your brand and your sales agent, and have them be assured that you will provide value to them. You lower cost in the CAC process by automating your follow up, positioning your brand well, and streamlining the process to deliver exactly what your prospects are looking for.

Success or failure will be determined by your ability to qualify leads and the ability to control your customer acquisition cost. If you are praying that you get a new client this week, next week or next month, you are walking on thin ice.

You must have at least 4 or 5 proven lead sources from which you can harvest leads. If those can be turned on and off as you need them, that's even better.

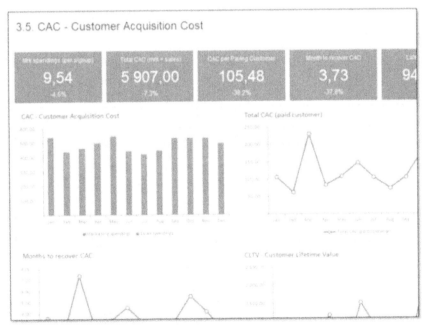

Above is an example of a Customer Acquisition Cost dashboard after which you could model yours.

You'll see that they have marketing spending per signup (or opt-in) in the top left, total marketing plus sales, the cost per paying customer, and so on.

Breaking these down very specifically will be the key to your success.

I'm only scratching the surface on what you need to know about getting prospects, turning them into paying clients and determining how much profit they will make you throughout their customer lifecycle. The detail needed to understand all of this can be overwhelming unless you have done it before, or you have a badass coach that knows what to look for and what to ignore.

When I ask my clients, "Do you know exactly where your sales are coming from?"

The most common answer I get is, "I do the sales; I know where my clients come from." Yet, without precise new lead data you can never know exactly where your best clients come from.

Getting referrals from your friend and family network is important, and a great way to obtain new business, but it's not something you can thrive on without any supplemental ways of finding new leads on your own. Getting new leads on your own proves you're a self-sustaining agency who can drive leads based on its talent and brand instead of because you "knew a guy who knew a guy." Now, if you're okay with only getting clients from your friend and family network, then ignore everything you've read. If you are ready to blow your agency up, then you better hold on to this and take some notes, because this is going to determine your success or failure.

Step 6: Developing New KPIs Module

Always keep your company's purpose, vision, mission, quality assurance, employee priorities, and profitability at the front of your brain when you're thinking about what you truly need to learn from your profit measuring tactics.

You want to bridge together all aspects of your business to avoid miscommunications and misunderstandings between your employees.

Once this data, your revision and leadership, automation tactics, marketing strategies, and the overall business operations are all cohesive and in agreement with one another, you'll be able to track your progress more smoothly.

Define the systems and processes involved; being a CEO doesn't ever get any easier.

You will be required to standardize things to make management easier and maintain your sanity. Give ownership to other people through delegation. Give those people everything they will need to accurately harvest the data you want them to collect.

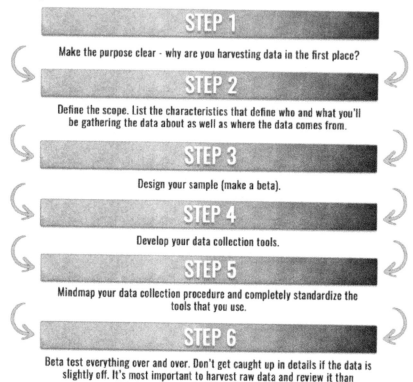

STEP 1
Make the purpose clear - why are you harvesting data in the first place?

STEP 2
Define the scope. List the characteristics that define who and what you'll be gathering the data about as well as where the data comes from.

STEP 3
Design your sample (make a beta).

STEP 4
Develop your data collection tools.

STEP 5
Mindmap your data collection procedure and completely standardize the tools that you use.

STEP 6
Beta test everything over and over. Don't get caught up in details if the data is slightly off. It's most important to harvest raw data and review it than it is to perfect it as it comes out of the gate.

Automation is ideal. "Closed-loop" data, or data that bridges the gap between sales and marketing, will be much more reliable and cost nothing once it's set up. Bridging the gap between the data collected by your sales team and the data collected by your marketing team will once again cause for less miscommunications and less misunderstandings.

Having more automated systems helps close the loop between your sales and marketing teams because the information each team gathers is shared in the cloud and can be edited and uploaded by both parties.

That way, you'll have one version of every document rather than 5 edited versions of a document with no clue as to which one is the most recently updated. In all, the more time you spend automating, the less time you'll be wasting doing everything by hand, and the more accurate your information will be. However, it is easier said than done. You should standardize everything. Simplify as much as possible if you want to truly break the glass ceiling your business is trapped underneath. **Develop meeting and reporting rhythm**.

People expect what you inspect. Hold people accountable to get the numbers to you. If you don't hold them accountable twice in a row, you can bank on the fact that they're not showing up for the third meeting. And that's your fault, not theirs.

Define your challenges.

Employee resistance is a common challenge. On occasion, people will fail you. You will give them a task, and they will not follow through. However, it's important to express the importance of all of this to all of your employees so they understand how the research about performance indicators benefits them and the company they work for. Your system won't always match up. Yes, technology will fail (or at least disappoint) you. You'll run some analytics once and it'll give you X result, but then you'll run it again, and you get Y result.

This is to be expected, though it is challenging.

Test, and test some more until you get cohesive data you can work with. Time and money become an issue. Time and money are clearly some "nonrenewable resources" that each business has to work with. This does make life harder on business owners, especially when some of this data doesn't reap much reward for close to a month—however, it's the wisest investment of time and money that can explain your past mistakes and prevent (a lot of) your future mistakes. The most important point to remember is this: performance indicators trump all of these to invest in long-term success. Plan for challenges like these and know that the value you get from tracking your data far surpasses any number of challenges you'll face along the way.

Develop a scorecard

This can manifest itself in many ways - you can give the people overseeing your performance indicators a physical grade and expect them to improve their grade over a certain period of time—thus, giving them their own performance indicators for you to evaluate.

Step 7: Managing Your KPIs

Assign ownership and relinquish control...

Look at what items you can hand over to other people. It is simply not possible to be the person gathering data and the person reviewing data. It's counterproductive to even try. In some cases, the leader is the only person capable of doing this-or-that thing, but delegate as much as possible. If you're creating the performance indicators, when it comes time to review them, too much information or bias can confuse you and make you come up with excuses as to why you're not hitting your goal. Remove yourself as much as possible. Everything you do should be with the intent to hand this off to someone else as soon as possible. Delegation is key to making your performance indicators work for you and mean something in the life of your business. **Make ownership very clear**

 Make sure you're expecting people to compile what you ask, but also to come up with creative ideas to solve those issues pointed out by performance indicators. Train them to expect more out of themselves as well as everyone around them. Force them to step up and be a true leader.

Praise and celebrate

Sometimes in business, things actually go right. Give your employees personal credit if the goals you all set together are actually met because your team managed to correctly monitor the performance indicators in place. Make it a company-wide celebration—really show them how big of an accomplishment this was and incentivize this behavior to continue.

Step 8: Business Intelligence

Business Intelligence, Real Time Performance Indicators Google Spreadsheets and Historical Trending --The longer they are tracked, Performance Indicators give you more and more insight into how to make your agency more efficient. That's why it is critical that you start a Google Spreadsheet and track everything and track it as often as you need.

For example, if payroll is every two weeks, then track the total payroll, taxes paid, and insurance payments every two weeks. If you make a loan payment once a month, then track it monthly.

If it's leads source tracking, you will want to track that weekly so you can stay on top of it. Use common sense when deciding on what to track and when to track it.

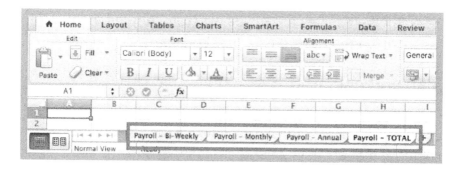

Like you see above, you will need to create a tab on the spreadsheet for each time frame you are tracking and one master tab that compiles all the data into a simple view for you and your leadership team to monitor and discuss. Something else to consider is real time performance indicators. These are ideal if you can get the right type of systems in place.

This requires having a customer relationship management platform and having your entire client path running through that CRM. Once this is in place you can use systems like Graphly, Wicked Reports and Amazon Quick Sights to monitor your agency's performance in real time.

Key Performance Indicators Wrap Up

We can all agree that none of us have any time to waste....

That being said, if you took the time to go through this book, you've got to do something with what you learned.

Seeing as taking your company to the next level is never easy, I'm not promising that it will be. But I can promise you that these methods work. I've seen them in action. I started using them in my first agency, carried them over to my coaching business, and now I coach other top-notch agencies all over the world on the same concepts, and they're working for them too.

Here are a few actionable items you can start with to transform the way your company tracks and recreates success:

Start a Google spreadsheet and give editing controls to the right people to start tracking your expenses, revenue, and customer acquisition costs.

Personally, break down every line item in great detail under each category, see how much each employee costs, each department costs, and how much revenue each employee brings in and each department brings in

There are many other ways you can take control of your agency by running based on numbers.

The more you get these in place, the more you can delegate and untether yourself from the day-to-day grind.

If you'd like to learn about any of these other concepts in more depth, do not hesitate to contact us.

MONTH ELEVEN

Learn how to position your agency to be the best and only choice among other digital marketing agencies.

Chapter 11

Brand Positioning

You are about to learn how to stand out and make it clear to new clients that you are the best choice. If followed correctly you will have the client base you've built since month one on a waiting list for your superior services!

Defined:

"The goal is to create a unique impression in the customer's mind so that the customer associates something specific and desirable with your brand that is distinct from the rest of the marketplace." – **Cult Branding**

"The act of designing the company's offerings and image to occupy a distinctive place in the mind of the target market." – **Kotler**

Essentially, brand positioning is what separates you from your competitors, builds value in your brand, and makes you the only choice as far as your target audience, or customer avatar is concerned. As you can see, it is very important to understand brand positioning and to have a game plan in place to ensure your agency is working toward being the only option for your target audience. Some of the items required to build a world-class brand positioning are easy, while others are harder to get in place. All of them require a strategy and a plan of attack.

That is why we like to call our workbook the Brand Positioning Vortex. In the beginning it doesn't have much pull on your target audience, but as the vortex grows, it grabs your target audience and does not let them go until they reach the center of the vortex (your agency).

Obviously, all agencies want their prospects to perceive their brand as the only choice, but exactly how do you get your agency to that level?

Well, in this chapter we are going to give you the exact items you need to get in place, help you create a brand positioning statement. When you are done with this section, you will have a clearly defined brand position statement, know exactly what items you need to get in place and have a plan of attack to get it all done.

Here is a visual representation my staff put together to give you an idea of how the brand positioning vortex works:

As I mentioned, brand positioning is similar to a vortex. A vortex does not have a lot of gravitational pull when it first forms (as you build your brand positioning), but as it grows in size and gets stronger (you have built a very strong brand positioning statement), the gravitational pull sucks everything (your prospects) down towards the center of the vortex (your agency).

Big advertising and marketing agencies are constantly preaching about brand penetration, but do not get these two things confused, they are completely different strategies.

One is about getting your name in front of millions of people consistently (brand penetration) and the other is influencing prospects' and clients' buying decisions (brand positioning). When you are in the process of building your agency, it is critical that you get a very strong brand positioning strategy in place.

You should constantly work toward increasing the influence, pressure, and pull you have on your prospects' buying decisions because it will help your agency convert more leads and convert them much faster.

Brand Penetration

≠ Brand position

If you are a smaller or newer agency you should focus your efforts on influencing your prospects' buying decisions with as much pressure and pull as possible. Concentrating on being influential and having impact on a few prospects is more important in this stage of business development than just putting your logo in front of a bunch of people, and the latter can cost you a fortune. This doesn't mean you can scrap your advertising budget, but you do have to find a healthy mix between the two.

To put things in perspective, think about it like this: would you rather get 50 leads a year and close 25 of them, or would you rather get 100 leads a year and close 25?

Remember it costs money to get every single lead, so you have to make a decision about which is more important to your agency, closing more of the leads you already get, or getting a lot more leads.

Brand positioning is so important because it helps you do more with less. In other words, you spend less on media buying and you close more big money projects. In the next few pages, we provide a brand positioning checklist. Read the next few pages and give your agency a physical grade on your brand positioning.

50%

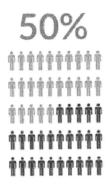

25 leads out of 50
at $1/lead = $50 for 25 leads
1 lead = $2

25%

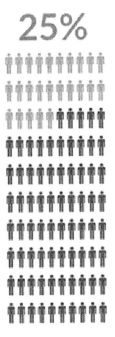

25 leads out of 100
at $1/lead = $100 for 25 leads
$1 lead = $4

Above is a brand positioning assets checklist of all the items you need to get in place to increase the brand positioning for your agency. Each item in this list has a description of what your agency would look like if that particular item deserves an "A" – so, if you feel that your agency's performance in that aspect of brand positioning measures up, give yourself an **"A." If you feel like you're nowhere close to having that item in place, give yourself an "F," and so on.** For now, just focus on grading your agency's performance. In the next section of the workbook we are going to help you determine what you should start working on now, and what can wait

- € **Differentiate Your Agency** – I am able to define in great detail why my agency is different from and better than my competitors. My agency has a dominant project management process that is 100% transparent, which separates me from competitors and brings value to my target audience, or customer avatar.

- € **Niche/Vertical Markets** – I am an expert at what I do and I dominate my space. I am confident that I'm on the right track to becoming the best digital agency in the world for my customer avatar. I do not attempt to do everything for everyone – I have a very particular set of skills for a very specific target audience and exclusively serve my niche

- € .**Define Who You Are** – I have such a strong sense of purpose that prospects never wonder what I stand for. I am not only in business for profit. Prospects gravitate toward my agency because of our strong sense of purpose – they can tell we are not an agency driven only by profits. My agency stands for something bigger, which increases our perceived value in our target audience's (or avatar's) eyes.

- € **Define Complexities** – We have what it takes to create powerful ads or a converting website for our clients. The complexities of our proven service process and highly skilled workforce are explained in detail to prospects and clients. We always let them know they are asking for something that is hard and it takes unbelievably talented individuals to do the project they're starting with us. We go to great lengths to make them realize that simply anybody can't do what we do, so that our prospects will have a deeper appreciation for our services.

€ **Transparent Communications** – We define our policies up front and in detail. We let them know what our refund policy is, what our service level agreement is, and we define it in clear and concise terms they can understand. We realize this actually adds value for the larger more sophisticated clientele. However, our transparency doesn't stop there, it continues throughout the entire project. Our project management processes provide clear details on billing processes, deliverable deadlines, etc.

€ **Low Trust Engagements** – We excel in getting our foot in the door, building trust and then graduating into the larger projects. If you can get your foot in the door with a lower priced strategic planning option, or a smaller project to build trust, it builds substantial brand credibility and positions your agency as the go to option for larger projects.

€ **Strong Digital Footprint** – It's easy for your prospects to find you or research your agency, because you have a positive and large digital footprint. You've got organic search engine optimization, plenty of press releases, a strong social media presence, many directory listings (BBB, Partner Directories, etc.), and so on.

€ **Social Proof** – You have several big-name testimonials. You give away free services to get video testimonials from admired figures in your local area or industry. You understand that many people find ads to be dishonest, which is why you supplement ads with real people talking positively about your product to be credible and trustworthy.

€ **Social Trust** – You have won awards in your specific niche or local area (these awards build tremendous value and allow you to increase your prices overnight). You have entered into the local newspapers "Best in Community" contests or go for the "Partner of the Year" in your specific partner community or you've gone big and won national publication awards like Entrepreneur Magazine. Your current situation can best be described as not IF your prospects want to hire you but was more about if they could afford to hire you. You've tried to pay for regional advertisements in big named magazines like Time or People, which you feature on your website as an "As seen in [INSERT PUBLICATION]" type of thing.

€ **Third Party/Big Name Endorsements** - You are in the position to get a well-known person or even a famous person to endorse you and be your spokesperson. People see celebrities endorsing your product, so they assume it must be high quality.

€ **Perceived Value** – You clearly describe every added benefit of working with you to your prospects and clients. You remind them why you're the best choice. Your presentations explode off of the page and tell stories behind why you are in business serving your target audience.

€ **Bring the Pain!** – You don't just deliver features. You position your services as a solution to your target audience's pain points. You let them know that what they are currently doing is not working and you give them a clearly defined solution that is going to fix their pain points.

Step 1: Brand Analysis

We have created a very simple 3 step process to help you determine exactly what your agency's brand positioning should focus on and how to get it implemented.

Target Audience Wants and Desires – You need to understand exactly what your target audience or customer avatar wants, and what their pain points are. Create a desire to fix it with your agency's services.

Brand Capabilities – The biggest lies we tell are the ones we tell ourselves, this applies to our agencies as well. You need to clearly define what you're capable of. Even if you build cheap   websites then own it. you are capable of building websites faster and cheaper than anyone else!

Competitive Analysis – Research, Secret Shop, and intimately understand how your competitors are positioning their brands/services.

Brand Capabilities

Target Audience

Competitive Analysis

Step 2: Create Your Brand Positioning Statement

Your brand positioning statement is internal language that guides your company's efforts. It is there to make sure everything you do aligns with how you want to be perceived by your target audience. It is important to keep the following things in mind when crafting your brand positioning statement

DIFFERENTIATE – What separates you from your competitors? People need to know why they should pick your agency over the competition. Figure out what makes your agency special or unique and use it to your advantage.

DELIVER – Can your agency be held accountable to deliver on your brand positioning statement? The claims you make need to be realistic and achievable.

BE MEMORABLE – Is it easy to remember? If it's going to govern your decisions, and more specifically marketing efforts, your staff needs to be able to easily remember what direction they're heading in.

SHOW POWER – Does every word count? This needs to provide guidance and inspiration in your agency for years to come. It needs to remind your staff that you're in business for (and because of) your consumers.

USE EXAMPLE FROM ZIPCAR: – To urban-dwelling, educated techno-savvy consumers, when you use Zipcar car-sharing service instead of owning a car, you save money while reducing your carbon footprint.

Step 3: Implementation Of Brand Assets

Now that you have gone through the first two phases of creating a brand positioning statement, you should have a simple statement that reflects your agency.

At this point you need to implement this new brand positioning statement and all other brand positioning items that received an "A" in the brand positioning checklist. We provided a worksheet that helps you create your positioning statement and keep track of what items will be added to marketing materials and what marketing materials need to be updated. Download that worksheet and get started adding brand value to your agency today!

he more items you get in place, the bigger and stronger your vortex will become. Every added asset will create a stronger pull, and before you know, it your target audience will be running to your agency to use your services.

This 'pull and persuasion' takes time though, so don't get frustrated if it doesn't happen overnight. As with many things in your agency, you'll have to let time do some of the heavy lifting, but it helps to have a plan in place and if you know what to target you can substantially speed this process up.

A goal without a plan is just a wish.

*There is a Goal Setting Worksheet link in the resources area. You'll see this worksheet pop up in several of our lessons because having a specific plan with actionable items is the key to success.

Pull up that worksheet and make some of your goals the items you gave an "F" grades from above.

Really think about how you're going to get them in place. Be S.M.A.R.T when setting these goals (specific, measurable, achievable, realistic, and time-bound) because although you want to set the bar high, you want to be able to achieve what you set out to do. Another important aspect to setting goals is that success begets success, so make sure you sprinkle in small wins among all of the big goals.

Getting Started:

Complete the checklist above (and be completely real with yourself – don't fluff anything up just to look good.) This only works when you're totally honest.

Brand Positioning Wrap Up

 Like I said above "A goal without a plan is just a wish."

Now that you have the ability to get the right tools to set your goals and position yourself in your niche, it is up to you to take make it clear to new clients that you are the best choice. Only the best!

MONTH TWELVE

This chapter will teach you over the course of month twelve how to build your value in the eyes of you clients so that you will continue to be the best option in your niche and set prices so that you will get paid for every second of your precious time!

Chapter 12

Pricing

Once you've created a business model so powerful that your prospects see you as the only choice in your niche the information below with get you paid what you are worth!

Introducing Yourself To Pricing

Pricing can be a very complex topic; it literally has hundreds of moving parts. Over the past 15 years of being an agency owner or coaching other agency owners, I have figured out that it boils down to 3 simple concepts: the **3 Ms of Pricing**.

This formula is simple to understand, and if followed will allow you to increase your pricing by at least 10-20% in the next 90 days, and eventually allow you to double and maybe even triple your prices

1) Market Value – What the market will command is largely determined by how and why you deliver value to your clients. Reality is, a lot of that value is merely perceived, and totally in your control. In this workbook I give you 15 specific examples of how to build tremendous market value in your agency's services.

2) Maturity – How mature is your agency when it comes to its marketing, sales, service and business development infrastructure? The definition of mature is: having completed natural growth and development. The keyword here is natural. Some things in life just take time and can only happen as your agency matures.

3) Model – What is your pricing model? There are 6 different types of pricing models you can select from – and I'll define each of them for you.

All three of the items above play a critical role in how much and how often you can charge for your services. The value you provide based upon client reporting and project management processes all play a big role. If you can say you have been in business for over 15 years and serviced over 3,000 clients globally you can obviously charge more than someone who is just getting started. As you can see, there are literally hundreds of variables that play a role in pricing. Fortunately for you, you already possess a lot of them, but you just didn't know you could leverage them – until today I'll teach you to understand the primary factors that play into pricing, which ones deserve your precious time, and what you should focus on right out of the gate so you can charge much more for your services.

Some factors take time and can only happen with your agency's maturity, but other things can be done quickly and take very little effort. As you go through this workbook and online program, pick the top 3-5 items you can have in place in the next 30-60 days. Knock those out and raise your prices by 10-20% NOW. Most agencies dramatically undervalue their services and should raise prices immediately.

Truth is, unfortunately, you may lose a client or two in the process. As an agency owner you're probably thinking, "But I need every penny from every client!"

That is true but let me finish.

In your agency about 10% of your clients are probably consuming 80-90% of your time.

You have been afraid to get rid of them because they have been with you for a long time and are a huge part of making payroll every month; your bread and butter clients.

But a crazy thing happens when you raise your prices: some customers will be upset and leave, but they tend to be the needy ones that consume most of your time.

The good news is: you raised your prices for the clients who are STILL on board (and COMING on board!), so you've increased your total gross revenue by 10- 15%.

This means that losing 5% of your clients will be more than made up by the higher prices. You need to be strategic when you increase your prices; we have found the best time to raise your prices is when you are going into a new year. So, in December, send out an email to your client base explaining to them that you are growing, and improving your service offerings.

As of (pick a date in January) your prices will increase from $ABC/hour to $XYZ/hour. If anyone would like to get anything done on the legacy pricing, they would need to start their projects BEFORE that date.

This does three things: it shows them that 1) your agency is awesome and in high demand, 2) you're improving your services (and therefore building more value), and 3) it gives your sales a massive boost in December.

As soon as your clients hear there will be a price increase, a lot of them will reach out and try to get as much done as possible under the legacy-pricing model.

Building Value Using Four Categories

1. Increase Demand

Increase your lead flow or revenue through delivering overwhelming value to your clients.

2. Provide Clarity

Provide clarity for your prospects or clients by providing a detailed project management process or a systematized method of delivering more effective Google Ads.

3. ROI/results

Provide your clients with detailed reporting on the results they will receive as a result of hiring your agency.

4. Perceived Value

This can be done in countless ways, but get started with world-class proposals, presentations, videos, social proof and social trust items.

Increase Demand

1. **Supply And Demand** –zents you want to work with. (Make sure to review our sales/marketing automation lesson and our lead generation lesson to get more leads and sales for your agency.)

2. **Over-deliver** – If your service is badass, and the word gets out that you're badass, you can charge whatever you want to charge.

3. **Become An Influencer** - Once you set the tone for digital marketing in your area, you're being sought after (now you can raise your prices!).

4. **Standardize** – Separate yourself from your competitors with proven, standardized systems that you can present during the sales cycle. Spend time documenting your service/deliverable process and be sure to replicate the methods that work.

5. **Accountable** – Make sure your agency is accountable for every action it takes; this is possible with a proven project management process. The ability to demonstrate accountability during the sales/service cycles adds tremendous value to your agency and validates why you have higher prices. A dedicated project manager, dedicated account manager, and an escalation process are a few of the ways to hold your agency accountable.

6. **Documentation** – Larger projects will require a detailed plan where all aspects of the project will need to be documented in great detail. At first this seems like a lot of work, but if you do it right it will be worth it because it is convenient for clients and shows you're detail oriented.

A good example is to offer a documented training manual on how to use a content management system.

ROI/Results

7. **Measurable** - Business owners will pay substantially more for your services if you provide detailed reporting, real time updates, and measured results. Larger organizations must be able to document and quantify everything to validate their budget expenses. If your agency is not providing measured results you will not get larger projects.

8. **Incentivize Your Staff** – Most agencies provide services based upon efficiency and that is perfectly fine. If you can sell based on the results (ROI) clients receive you can charge double or even triple. Obviously, this puts a lot more risk on your agency to perform at a higher level. So to mitigate that risk you will need to incentivize your staff to ensure they are dedicated to producing results. If they exceed expectations, there will be rewards, and if they fall short, there will be consequences.

Perceived Value:

9. **Raise Your Prices Right Now!** - Most digital marketing agencies aren't charging enough for the work they do. Starting right now, charge 10-20% more for what you're currently offering.

10. **Waiting List** – Even if you do not need a waiting list, it is a good idea to build up perceived value by placing prospects on a waiting list. Now we only did this when there was a need to throttle how much project work was being dumped into the service department. So if you just landed a ton of big projects, place the next few that come in on a waiting list and ask them to put down a retainer fee to hold their spots. Then when it comes time to bid on the project, bump your prices up.

11. **Brand Positioning** – There are tons of things you can do to position your brand as the go-to choice for your local area, partner community or niche. I will scratch the surface of positioning in this workbook, but if you want to do a deep dive, make sure to go through our Brand Positioning lesson. A few basic things you can do to increase your brand position will be social proof, social trust, or celebrity endorsements.

Remember: celebrity endorsements can be your local mayor; it does not have to be a Hollywood celebrity.

12. **Value Proposition** – You have to be able to define your agency's value proposition in clear and compelling terms. What, in extreme detail, are you providing that is so worth the higher price? List every little detail. We, as owners, take the obvious things for granted, but your prospects don't realize what is obvious and what isn't. Build up your list of offerings.

13. **Perceived Value** – The better you illustrate, define, and spruce up your brand image the more perceived value it will have. There is a fine line between fluff and value. To put this in perspective I'll give an example. A jewelry designer sold emerald necklaces for $40 each, but nobody was buying them. She told her manager to discount them to $20, but the manager accidentally changed it to $200. Suddenly the necklaces flew off the shelves because people assumed they were higher quality. (Why do you think Apple products are so expensive?)

14. **Demonstrate Level Of Effort** (LOE) – Sometimes clients don't know what it takes to complete a specific aspect of a project. For example, to complete a world-class design you must create a model, define brand pillars, determine target audiences, and create a proof of concept. Plus, all of this has to happen before an actual conceptual can even be created. Define exactly what it will take to get the world-class results they desire. Once your clients understand the amount of effort involved they will have a greater respect for the amount of work you put into their project. Again, don't take the "obvious" things for granted. Spell it out.

15. TOTAL CUSTOMER LIFECYCLE

- Build out a client path that allows you to monetize all aspects of the client relationship. One way to do this is to sell a strategic planning phase before the larger project. Or for clients who are not quite ready for a big website or monthly media buying retainer, have a low trust engagement to get them into the basket.

16. DEVELOPING YOUR BUSINESS

The first thing all agency owners must consider is their agency's maturity in regard to business development. How sophisticated is your agency? Have you serviced Fortune 500 companies? Do you have more leads than you can handle? Have you won countless awards? Have you been in business for 15+ years and been endorsed by celebrities? For most people, the answer to all of those is NO.

The 3 primary steps in business development:

1. START UP – Generally, start up mode coincides with survival mode. So a lot of the recommendations in this workbook will take you a while to get in place. For all agencies in this phase of business development it is critical that you dedicate time to all of these recommendations. This can prevent you from getting stuck in the vicious cycle of "see project, do project, and pray for the next project." I have been in that place before and it's painful. Think of these as requirements, not mere recommendations or suggestions.

2. AWKWARD GROWTH – This phase can be frustrating because this is what holds the majority of agencies back from breaking through their glass ceiling. Agencies in this phase have typically been in business for a few years, their average annual revenue is around $350K – $750K with around 7-15 employees. These agencies are experiencing the hard reality that the owners alone cannot do everything themselves if they want to break through the 7-figure mark. They must learn to transition out of their current role (even if they love what they're doing) and step into the role of a true CEO and leader.

3. MATURE AGENCY – Agencies in this phase are at a level that most people would consider to be successful. They average $750K-$3M in revenue, have been in business for 8+ years, and have 20+ employees. Maturity brings in its own list of new problems. This is when you need to consider bringing in celebrity endorsements, establish a full time marketing and sales department, and take your agency performance indicators to a more granular level.

The Different Types Of Pricing:

FIXED BID – Fixed bid projects can be extremely profitable, but they can also put you into bankruptcy if they're not documented properly. I have never met a client who did not go out of their way to squeeze as much work as possible out of a fixed bid project.

A good way to get around fixed bid projects is to either develop it into a niched-out package deal (I'm a big fan of these) and/or correlate every task on a project into an hourly estimate.

If you associate each task to an hourly estimated time of completion and the client demands you include advanced functionality as a part of that task, you can simply remind them that you can do it, but you are associating this back to an hourly estimate and they will be responsible for overages.

CHANGE ORDER

Date:	***INSERT DATA HERE***
Project:	***INSERT DATA HERE***
Change Order #:	***INSERT DATA HERE***

TYPE OF CHANGE ORDER (Check one:)

☒ Standard Change Order
☐ Unforeseen Site Condition (Justification
☐ Emergency (Authorization attached)
☐ Substantial (Authorization attached)

Description of Change:

The following Proposed Change Order(s) are incorporated into the Contract by reference:

Ref. #	Summary Description:	Amount:	Initiated by:
Original Contract Amount:			
Previous Change Order(s):			
Contract Amount Prior to this Change Order:			
Amount of this Change Order:			
New Contract Amount Including this Change Order:			

In effect, by correlating every task to an hourly estimate you turn the project into an hourly project, and therefore protect your agency from huge scope creep overages. If you do the hourly correlation, make SURE the client understands this up front. If they want additional or advanced features it will most likely cause additional fees or charges.

If you can't tell, I am not a big fan of fixed bid projects without a safeguard in place for your agency. I understand the necessity of giving a fixed bid on certain projects, but I would strongly advise to keep fixed bid projects limited to smaller projects, implementing a charge order process, and creating a very detailed scope document at the beginning of the project. Although if you do use the fixed bid model, you need to turn it into either a package deal or an hourly deal as a result of a detailed scope document and change orders.

HOURLY – This one typically works well, but can cause points of conflict with your clients. We found it best to sell blocks of hours and then let the clients know that when those hours run out, they will be billed for another block of hours. Each block should have predefined milestones, and your service department should do everything possible to hit those milestones. This way of billing tends to be the safer route. You are protected from scope creep and legal liability because you are billing in smaller amounts.

MONTHLY RETAINER – This can be manifested in many ways: the most common ways are for traffic generation services and social media services. A less common way is to provide an on demand service for your clients based on their needs and your service bandwidth. In all of these ways, most of the risk falls within in the first few months. This is because generally the bulk of the work is done to get everything set up, and once it is set up they are billed automatically. Then, your profit margins go up substantially! There needs to be strict legal documents in place that outline the deliverables and the client's responsibilities.

VALUE BASED – This pricing model is great because it's based on the amount of value the products and services bring the client. A lot of times, these manifest themselves into a package type of services or a canned program. Instead of charging hourly or on a percentage of ad spend, you charge for a program that delivers overwhelming value as a result of a trade secret, patent, or dominant offering over your competitors. This is particularly common in niche markets. An example would be an educational program for financial advisors that is canned but can't be found anywhere else. You could charge substantially more for that program because of its uniqueness and intellectual value.

RESULTS (ROI) BASED - This pricing model can be very risky, but it can also be very rewarding and profitable. If you decide to use this method make sure you base it on metrics that are easily quantifiable. So, don't make it based on how big the deals their sales staff are closing.

You should structure it under a predefined customer lifecycle value. For example, for every 20 additional leads your company receives, 1 will convert and become a new client.

For every new client won an average of $10,000 will come into the company over a six-month period. This is a predefined formula that you can quantify, measure, and achieve. Only take this course of action if you are certain you can deliver, and you are confident in the client's abilities and services.

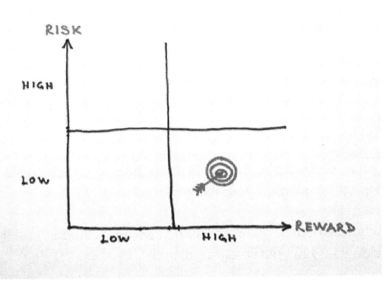

PACKAGE DEALS – Package deals are typically done in two formats but can obviously be applied to any number of package offerings. The first is a "menu item" type of package and the second is a "vertical/niche market" package. Menu item is a type of package where you offer a 10-page website with custom graphics for $3,995.00 or a Google Adwords management campaign for a $2,500.00 setup. The second type is the vertical/niche package where you offer a specific package for specific needs in a niche or industry.

This is a package custom tailored for lawyers, plumbers, doctors, etc. Everything included in the package is geared towards that industry's specific needs and requirements.

You can't increase the value of your brand overnight, but you can definitely get started sooner rather than later. To start out, look at your website and see how you can build your social trust and social proof to your prospects.

Are there places you can feature five star ratings and reviews?
Do you have testimonials from big name clients or local celebrities?

Why not, make a plan to obtain those as soon as possible and get them all over your website.

Look at your email campaigns and see how you can better provide value to your target audience.

Collect testimonials, reviews, and 5-star ratings to feature on your website

Raise your prices by at least 20% RIGHT NOW

Edit the sales copy on all of your collateral to explain in extreme detail the benefits of working with your agency.

Foster a connection with a local celebrity or big name in your community to get an endorsement that is featured on your website

The above tasks are just a few things you can do to get started.

Again, your market value cannot be raised overnight, but your prices sure can!

Pricing Wrap Up

 As soon as you finish this lesson, raise your prices by 20%...

Yes, really. And make some forward movement on your collateral explaining the incredible value you provide to your clients.

As always, we are here to serve.

If you have any questions, comments, or concerns about pricing or any other topic we cover, please don't hesitate to send us an email at info@leegoff.com.

Below is are the links to one-on-one counseling, webinars, resources and more that are mentioned throughout the book- - that will help you on your way to success...

RESOURCES

Free Agency Success Roadmap Webinar Series

Follow along with this monthly companion webinar series each month, as you read this book, and travel down your personal roadmap to success. Over the year you will be able to learn more about the cost-effective, sustainable solutions, that are included within these pages. This free webinar series is designed to educate agency owners on the best practices available to them and empower them to really focus on the details that are so important to succeeding.

Sign-up here:
https://agencysuccessroadmap.com/webinar/

Agency Success Roadmap Group Coaching Program

If your goal is to be a better agency owner consider the breakthroughs possible if you worked with a coach that uses a combination of strong business experience plus detailed coaching skills to help you take your agency to the next level.

Gain team building skills while getting a hand up on agency business development with proven, simple, step by step actions.

Including:

Two Dedicated Webinars A Month

One incredible educational webinar where we really get into the details of the tools and decisions you should consider when making on the topics for that month.

Each month during the second webinar we will do follow-up, answer questions, and go through a few examples with different group members.

There will be no more than 40 agency owners in each group and each group is paired up with other agency owners in similar positions (we do our best here)

PLUS+ You personally will receive TWO one-on-one Coaching Sessions per year.

On top of that you'll get <u>all</u> tools and templates mentioned in this book and more at:
https://agencysuccessroadmap.com/group/

Online Courses and Coaching Programs

If you are looking for the extra proposals and templates we mentioned in this book here is the link!

You will find templates, guides & tools to assist you to build your knowledge on a range of agency business topics here:

https://marketingagencycoach.com/digital-marketing-agency-coaching-programs-and-online-courses/

70800590R00166

Made in the USA
Columbia, SC
25 August 2019